Pulp Friction

Blaise Cronin

The Scarecrow Press, Inc.
Lanham, Maryland and Oxford
2003

SCARECROW PRESS, INC.

Published in the United States of America
by Scarecrow Press, Inc.
A Member of the Rowman & Littlefield Publishing Group
4720 Boston Way
Lanham, Maryland 20706
www.scarecrowpress.com

PO Box 317
Oxford
OX2 9RU, UK

British Cataloguing in Publication Information Available

Library of Congress Cataloging-in-Publication Data

Cronin, Blaise.
    Pulp friction /Blaise Cronin,
        p. cm.
    Includes bibliographical references.
    ISBN 0-8108-4547-4 (alk. paper)
        1. Library science. 2. Information science. I. Title.

Z665 .C78 2003
020—dc21

2002030575

Printed in the United States of America

⊗™ The paper used in this publication meets the minimum requirements
of American National Standard for Information Sciences—Permanence of
Paper for Printed Library Materials, ANSI/NISO Z39.48-1992.

To Ken Gros Louis

Philistinism is always active, always taking new forms, the New Philistinism vigorous under the guise of feminism, racism, elitism, imaginary concepts really pledged, not to their alleged aims (in fact often precisely the reverse, especially racism) but anarchy, attack on critical values, classical forms.

—Anthony Powell

CONTENTS

CREDITS

The works listed immediately hereafter originally appeared in *Library Journal* (in some cases with very minor word changes as a result of copy-editing decisions). They are reprinted here with permission. Copyright 2000, 2001, and 2002 Cahners Business Information, a division of Reed Elsevier Inc. "Accreditation: Retool It or Kill It," "Whatever Happened to Common Sense?" "Customer Satisfaction," "Rank Injustice?" "For Whom the Bell Curve Tolls," "The Mother of All Myths," "The View from the Trenches," "The Dreaded 'L' Word," "Process Fetish," "A Safe Haven," "A Community Intelligence Service," "Peer Review and the Stuff of Scholarship," "The End of First Sale," "Amazons R Us," "Margaret Rufsvold, Pioneer," "The Digital Divide," "The University Press," "Locus Classicus," "Milquetoast and Cookies," "Information Warfare," and "Welcome to My Web World."

"The Knowledge Management Drug" was extracted from a full-length article, "Knowledge Management, Organizational Culture and Anglo-American Higher Education," which was published in the *Journal of Information Science* 27, no. 3 (2001): 129–37 and is reprinted here with permission of Bowker and the Institute of Information Scientists.

"Digibabble" was originally published as "Digibabble (Letter from America)" in the *International Journal of Information Management* 18, no. 1 (1998): 73–74, and is reprinted here with permission from Elsevier Science.

"Quis Custodiet Ipsos Custodes?" was originally published as "Quis Custodiet Custodes? (Letter from America)" in the *International Journal of Information Management* 20, no. 4 (2000): 311–13, and is reprinted here with permission from Elsevier Science.

PREFACE

This svelte volume draws together a selection of opinion and other pieces I have published in the past few years. It also includes several essays and afterthoughts that have not previously seen the light of day. Some of the material was written originally for the "Dean's List" column in *Library Journal* (*LJ*), and I am most grateful to *LJ*'s editor-in-chief, John Berry III, and his colleagues—not to mention Norman Horrocks of Scarecrow Press who acted as matchmaker—for providing me with a bully pulpit, since my views and theirs have occasionally been known to differ. It is fun to pontificate in print, particularly from one's privileged perch in the groves of academe and, I dare say, it's a lot easier than making things work day in, day out in the world of professional practice.

One of the especially satisfying aspects of writing for *LJ*, given its estimated 100,000 readership, is that even the blandest piece manages to incite some kind of reaction. I have received plenty of plaudits and bytes of bile, both publicly in *LJ*'s letters column and privately via e-mail. The good news is that some of my jottings have had some effect, even if, on occasion, I have found myself being patted on the back both by individuals and organizations with whom I imagine (nay trust) I have little in common, while in other cases those with whom I have naïvely assumed a common bond have sometimes been among the most discombobulated of the magazine's readership.

It would be artificial to retrofit a unifying theme to these forty-plus short essays and obiter dicta. Some are polemical, some didactic, others ruminative in character. But I trust that they are not seen as an instance of what Richard Posner (2001, 299) terms the "declinist genre"—a lament for the loss of a professional Eden. That said, the collation does have an underlying purpose, namely, to joust with

the shibboleths and fashionable assumptions that characterize contemporary thinking in "Libraryland." (For a brief excursus on the
derivation of the term, see "The Dreaded 'L' Word" in this volume.)
Even after more than a decade in this country, I remain bemused by
my professional peers' fondness for tergiversation, to say nothing of
the increasingly pietistic clucking of the East Huron Street curia. It's
not just that we see the world differently, but that some of the positions taken by professional librarians, library science faculty, and
representatives of the American Library Association (ALA) are quite
simply lacking in basic common sense (see, for example, "Whatever
Happened to Common Sense?").

These are issues that I have explored elsewhere, notably in the
pugilistic "Shibboleth and Substance in North American Library
and Information Science Education," which was published in *Libri*
(45, no. 1 [1995]: 45–63). That paper, delivered originally as a keynote
address at the 1995 ALISE (Association for Library and Information
Science Education) annual conference, provoked frothy editorial reaction from both *Library Journal* ("Confronting Cronin's Complaint")
and *Progressive Librarian* ("A Blaise with Indignation"). Both editorials, particularly John Buschman's witty rebuttal in *Progressive Librarian* (10/11 [Winter 1995/96]: 1–2), deserve to be read in the interests of fair play. So, too, Chris Atton's lengthier, if humorless,
rejoinder in *Libri* (47, no. 2 [1997]: 101–106), "Against Blaise Cronin's
'Strategic Pragmatism' and in Defense of Social Responsibility in Librarianship." Masochists may also like to read the relevant parts of
John M. Budd's self-serving "Instances of Ideology in Discursive
Practice: Implications for Library and Information Science," which
appeared in the *Library Quarterly* (71, no. 4 [2001]: 498–517).

In many regards, the present miscellany is the progeny of that
Libri article, and constitutes a continuing, if necessarily marginal, effort on my part to ensure that heterodox views get a decent airing.
Since the world moves on, I have added postscripts to several
pieces, tweaked a few oversimplifications, and reflected on some of
the feedback I have received.

Several of the essays were generously critiqued by colleagues and
friends. It need hardly be said that providing feedback is not the same
thing as endorsing content, so, with that caveat clearly in mind, I'd like
to acknowledge the many sensible suggestions I received—including
those I gleefully ignored—from Elisabeth Davenport, Susan Herring, Rob Kling, Alice Robbin, Howard Rosenbaum, Debora Shaw,
and Reyes Vila-Belda.

Most especially, however, I should like to acknowledge the considerable personal debt I owe to Indiana University's sometime vice president for academic affairs and Bloomington chancellor of more than twenty years, Kenneth R. R. Gros Louis, whose sagacity and humanity exemplify the finest traditions of the North American higher education system, a system that, its well-documented shortcomings notwithstanding (see, for instance, "Postmodern Periphrasis"), remains the rightful envy of the civilized world.

REFERENCE

Posner, R. A. *Public Intellectuals: A Study of Decline.* Cambridge, Mass.: Harvard University Press, 2001.

ACCREDITATION:
RETOOL IT OR KILL IT

Originally published June 2000

As so often, Jesse Shera was on the mark. His words of nearly thirty years ago ring true today: "Library school accreditation doesn't scare anybody, except, of course, those who see what it may be doing to the profession." The latest brouhaha (see John Berry III's editorial of March 15, 2000, in *Library Journal*) has to do with variable reaccreditation rates. Since the introduction of the American Library Association's (ALA) 1992 *Standards for Accreditation*, almost one-third of programs seeking reaccreditation have received renewals of less than the full seven years. Some programs have been renewed for three years, some for four, and others for two and a half and five and a half. This is the kind of thing that would have brought tears of joy to medieval schoolmen weary of counting angels on pinheads.

What subtle distinctions make a program reaccreditable for, say, five rather than five and a half, or three rather than four years? The answer is, we don't know. And we don't know because neither the Committee on Accreditation (COA) nor the Office for Accreditation cares to tell us. Specifically, they won't divulge the criteria on which their highly nuanced decisions are based; this, of course, presupposes that there are explicit and consistently applied criteria, but like the scholastic philosophers' angels, they have yet to be seen. And remember: this is the American Library Association, the organization whose central tenet—its defining value proposition, if you will—is freedom of information. I'm sure that the irony would not have been lost on Shera. Imagine you're a graduate student in my class and I award you a grade of B- for your term paper, but provide no explanation of (a) what kind of work typically warrants a B- and (b) why your particular submission deserved such a grade. It's unthinkable. But apparently it's not unthinkable for those concerned with accrediting library and information science (LIS) programs.

1

This isn't simply a case of ruffled feathers or dented amour propre on the part of educators. Recent developments need to be understood in the larger historical context, namely, the damaging effect of current and recent COA practices on the long-term viability of library and information science as an acknowledged domain of academic endeavor.

The link between library school closings and accreditation was hypothesized by Tefko Saracevic six years ago in a cogently argued paper ("Closing of Library Schools in North America: What Role Accreditation?). An earlier version of that paper was posted on JESSE, the LIS educators' listserv, where, as I recall, it generated depressingly little reaction at the time (listserv aficionados will, however, be aware that traffic density on JESSE is proportional to topic triviality). Saracevic's paper described compellingly how "the iron grip model" of accreditation (his term) has resulted in a robotic rehearsal of elaborately stated objectives and a persistent avoidance of discussion, or definition, of the discipline's theoretical foundations. To make matters worse, this regressive practice was compounded by the COA's subsequent embrace of "political correctness." The net effect of these trends has been a dispiriting homogenization of LIS schools' accreditation rhetoric (just read any of the compendious self-studies, or program presentations as they're now called, if you don't believe me) and an uncritical veneration of vocationalism, fuzzy values, and process.

This concoction, unfortunately, does not go down well in research universities. "Who cares?" I can hear you say. If the Columbias and Chicagos of this world don't want their library schools, then so be it. Such smugness is distressingly myopic. The major, private universities no longer have library schools, and if Berkeley is anything to go by, the same may one day hold for the major public research universities. As Saracevic said, elite institutions consider library schools "vocational, irrelevant, and replaceable." Imagine, for a moment, a world in which LIS schools like Illinois, Indiana, and UCLA no longer existed. What sort of message would that send to the wider world? If library science were something taught at trade schools, would the brightest and best still consider entering the profession? If they spurned librarianship, what, ultimately, would be the effect on the quality of library services and occupational image?

If LIS schools in the major public research universities were shuttered, the profession would never recover. To be blunt, librarianship would become a second-class profession. The COA should recognize that our doors will remain open only if we conform to the academic and research norms of our host institutions, and if we demonstrate our willingness to evolve as a disciplinary community. Introversion and atavisim are the collective kiss of death within academia. Our greatest threat comes not from our parent institutions or from the emergence of new competitor schools outside the traditional LIS arena—and there are plenty of those—but from the COA. The COA's actions and words, as Shera, Saracevic, and others, myself included, have repeatedly observed over the years, threaten the viability of the very field that the ALA paradoxically purports to protect.

What's the solution? Quite a few of us, LIS administrators and faculty, would like to see accreditation eliminated or radically revised. Again, back to Shera, who noted that the COA had "tended to accredit 'from the bottom,' rather than 'from the top,' thus focusing attention on the minimum rather than the optimum." Accreditation adds no value whatsoever to our activities; in fact, it inhibits innovation, dissipates resources, and promotes posturing. It also invites the disdain of university presidents and provosts. Those of us working in major research institutions have our programs reviewed intramurally as a matter of course, ensuring that shoddy operations will be exposed. We don't need the interference of more or less well-intentioned outsiders to keep our houses in order.

So, where do we go from here? There are several options: (a) stick with the status quo and progressively dumb down the profession; (b) transfer responsibility for accreditation from the COA to some other body; (c) lay LIS accreditation firmly to rest; (d) reengineer the overall process, making it more transparent; and (e) move away from accrediting academic programs to accrediting libraries. The first is unacceptable. The second is feasible. The third is wishful thinking. The fourth is commonsensical. And the fifth . . .

REFERENCES

Saracevic, T. "Closing of Library Schools in North America: What Role Accreditation? *Libri* 44, no. 3 (1994): 190–200.

Shera, J. H. *The Foundations of Education for Librarianship.* New York: Becker and Hayes, 1972.

QUIS CUSTODIET IPSOS CUSTODES?

Originally published August 2000

In North America, there are more than fifty master's programs in library and information studies (often referred to as "MLS programs") accredited by the Committee on Accreditation (COA) of the American Library Association (ALA). Historically, the MLS, like the MBA for students of business, has been the passport to the world of professional practice. The role of the COA is to vet MLS programs seeking (re)accreditation and ensure that the requirements and expectations of the profession are being met. As is the case in many other fields, the views of the academic and professional communities on the value of accreditation are often polarized. Nothing new in that, of course (Saracevic 1994). However, the growing multidisciplinarity of library and information science (LIS) schools, reflected most dramatically in the influx of faculty from mainstream academic disciplines (e.g., computer science, psychology, sociology, communications) is fundamentally altering the ethos of some leading programs (Cronin 1995). Previously, LIS schools were culturally homogeneous: most faculty had doctorates in library and information science, and most acknowledged the professional character of their programs. Coextensive with the admission of "outsiders" has been an expansion of the degrees offered by LIS schools, and weaker coupling with the profession. In some cases, the MLS is only one of several degrees from which students can choose and, as a rule, these cognate degrees do not need accreditation from a professional body. As schools broaden their conceptual horizons and conform more to scholarly than professional norms, the friction between academia and the profession is intensifying. Recent discussion on accreditation in general, and on renewal decisions in particular, reveals a high level of mutual distrust.

Until the introduction of the COA's 1992 *Standards for Accreditation of Master's Programs in Library and Information Studies*, schools, if

4

reaccredited, were typically granted a seven-year renewal. The COA might still expect some changes to be made and require that schools report on progress, but the tacit expectation was that reaccreditation meant seven years. Reviews of programs under the current standards began in 1994, and as a result of the fifty-four decisions made to date:

- Thirty-six programs will be reviewed seven years after the COA decision
- One program will be reviewed five and a half years after the COA decision
- Six programs will be reviewed five years after the COA decision
- Five programs will be reviewed four years after the COA decision
- Four programs will be reviewed three years after the COA decision
- One program will be reviewed two and a half years after the COA decision
- One program had accreditation withdrawn, currently under appeal

The change in practice is striking. Many high-ranking programs, including some at the most prestigious universities, have been reaccredited for less than the full seven-year period. As a result, many deans and directors of LIS program have voiced serious disquiet about variable reaccreditation periods, both publicly and privately. Criticisms of the process were echoed in the June 1999 Report of the Congress for Professional Education (www.ala.org/congress /cope_report.html), which noted that "more than one third of programs reviewed now receive fewer than the full term between external on-site reviews yet no information is provided." Administrators are provided with no explanation as to why their programs are renewed for a given period. It is impossible to gauge from the feedback provided by the COA why a program has been granted a renewal period of, say, three or four rather than five or five and one-half years. Nor is it possible to deduce from the COA's comments what remedial steps would need to be taken to secure a longer renewal. Despite requests, the COA has not made public the criteria that it uses in determining renewal periods, nor provided assurances to the various stakeholders in the process that the criteria have been, and continue to be, applied consistently. This is anomalous. In academia, students are given grades for their work: faculty, students, and the public know what kind of work is required to earn an A+ or a B-. Grades are explicitly linked to demonstrable performance. And not just in academia: ice skaters know that failure to complete certain technical requirements (a double axle) will result in an automatic lowering of their mark, while a successful quad will push up the final score. None of this is meant to suggest that the process of grading is devoid of residual subjectivity, but the individual being rated does at least have a sense of what is expected and how his or her performance is likely to be calibrated. Not so with the COA. Given the centrality of accreditation to the reputations and, ultimately, the financial viability of MLS programs, it is not unreasonable for academic administrators to expect a clear statement of the criteria used in the re-accreditation calculus. Several questions require answer if concerns about procedural opacity are to be dispelled:

- Why variable renewal rates?
- What are the criteria upon which renewal decisions are based?
- How are the criteria translated into variable renewal periods?
- Why no clarification for the affected schools/programs?
- Why no clear information for the public?
- What purpose is the process serving, if neither producers nor consumers are fully informed of decisions and the bases on which they are made?

From the perspective of academic administrators, this issue has material significance. A program which is reaccredited for, say, three rather than seven years, may be perceived to be weak, or under threat: a short renewal period may well be equated in the consumer's mind with a riskier investment. The issue also has considerable symbolic import. The central tenet of the American Library Association is open and unfettered access to information, yet the COA's communications with its various constituencies are clearly at odds with this axial principle. The present situation goes well beyond the usual debate on the merits and demerits of accreditation in the LIS field. The lack of transparency in the process invites speculation as to the underlying motivations of the COA, and, by extension, the profession that it represents. As LIS programs broaden their intellectual bases and diversify both their faculties and curricula, it appears that representatives of the profession are signaling disapproval. It is as if variable renewal is a sanction that can be applied to rein in programs that seem to be veering off the straight and narrow. Unless the questions listed above are addressed convincingly by the COA, the mutual distrust that characterizes current LIS discourse in North America may provoke an irreparable schism within the ranks.

REFERENCES

Cronin, B. "Shibboleth and Substance in North American Library and Information Science Education." *Libri* 45, no. 1 (1995): 45–63.

Saracevic, T. "Closing of Library Schools in North America: What Role Accreditation?" *Libri* 44, no. 3 (1994): 190–200.

ACCREDITATION ANEW

In the *LJ* article, I identified five options for dealing with accreditation. These ranged from outright abolition, my continuing personal preference, to removing accreditation from the claws of the COA and placing it in the hands of another (as yet unspecified) body. In the intervening period, the ALA, acting on a recommendation from the 1999 Congress on Professional Education, established a task force to assess the desirability and feasibility of establishing an accrediting body external to the ALA (www.ala.org/congress/accredtf/index.html). The rationale was simple: the programs located in LIS schools are becoming increasingly diverse, while programs in allied information domains are drawing closer to those in the LIS community. Given these parallel trends, namely expansion and convergence, why not create an umbrella accrediting group to better reflect programmatic pluralism?

By April 2001, the task force had produced a draft proposal for external accreditation that recommended the creation of a 501(c)3 organization capable of providing program accreditation for any segment of the information professions. The organization would be a federation comprising such groups as the American Library Association, American Society for Information Science and Technology, Society of American Archivists, and the Special Libraries Association. I'll spare you the details regarding structure, governance, and finance. Suffice it to say that such a body would be only marginally better than the status quo, and then only because the current organization—the COA—is perceived to be, and here I'm quoting from the task force's draft document, "closed and relatively impervious to the changes occurring in the external environment."

Will this federation fly? I have my doubts. As I write this, the deans and directors of LIS programs have roundly criticized the proposal, and it may well be that it is dead in the water. Whatever the eventual outcome, one thing seems certain: the cost of support-ing this pumped-up beast would presumably be even greater than the present. COA. It's also safe to assume that the net increase in as-sociated bureaucratic costs would be passed on to programs seeking accreditation, such as mine. That is a thoroughly depressing prospect, one that merely adds insult to injury.

Uporn My Word!

You call it pornography, they call it adult entertainment. Whatever the label, sex sells. And how! Global estimates of the legal sex industry, which includes magazines, striptease clubs, phone sex, videos, and websites, is about $60 billion, or more than twice Disney's global earnings from all of its diversified businesses. The United States may account for $15 billion of the total, of which, in turn, video sales and rentals (approximately 700 million per year) alone account for $4 billion. To put things in perspective, revenues for sex goods and services are considerably larger than all movie box office receipts in this country. The adult entertainment sector is also more economically significant than the performing arts or, for that matter, than professional sports such as football and basketball. In the United States, Web-based pornography is estimated to be generating annual revenues in the $1 billion range. It is the one form of Internet content that seems (almost) recession proof. Claims such as these are ten a penny but, as I have also discovered, there is much skepticism in the air. Such is the nature of the industry, and such are the difficulties of measuring "adult content" online, that some of these frequently recycled numbers may be very inflated. But even if we halve the estimates above, we're still dealing with a significant social phenomenon.

Tens of millions of Americans surf sex sites, from home and work, though corporate surveillance is having a dampening effect on the latter; about one in three people who work online are being monitored. Established market research firms like Nielsen and Jupiter Media Metrix track in-home use of sex sites on the Web, and others, like Sextracker (www.sextracker.com) provide publicly accessible data on the daily hit rates of adult entertainment sites (broken down by time and category), as well as basic details of many of the companies being tracked. This, it should be noted, is not an exclusively American phenomenon. In June 2001, according to NetValue, an estimated 5.3 million Germans, 3.8 million Brits, and 2.7 million French citizens visited sex sites. The Germans spent more hours (in absolute terms) viewing online adult entertainment sites than any other nation, while Spaniards spent the highest proportion of their total online time surfing sex sites. Our antipodean cousins are no less keen: according to Media Metrix, a third of Australia's 6.8 million Internet users accessed adult entertainment sites in December 2000. Intriguingly, the growth in demand is not limited to consumers; the number of free adult entertainment sites is estimated to be more than a quarter of a million. In other words, a lot of individuals (men and, increasingly, women) are getting their kicks from developing, presenting, and distributing, as opposed to consuming, pornographic images and paraphernalia.

And it's not just in our bedrooms and offices that we're sampling porn. Hotels have become a major distribution channel. Forty percent of all U.S. hotel rooms now offer adult materials, typically videos, to their guests, and not a few hotel guests (I've seen figures ranging from 10 to 50 percent) purchase such materials. These, and other statistics, even allowing for some degree of sampling error, paint a striking picture of contemporary mores. The consumption of pornography is neither an economically minor nor socially marginal activity in the United States, despite the fact that the subject is rarely addressed in polite (e.g., academic) circles. The data suggest that we may be witnessing the mainstreaming of pornography (Cronin and Davenport 2001).

The image of the pornographer is also changing. The characters who populated the movie *Boogie Nights* are giving way to, on the one hand, the arch amateur (which helps explain the thousands of free websites) and, on the other, CPAs and corporate executives bristling with MBAs. Nor does the male-dominated stereotype hold so strongly: more and more women are involved in the design, development, operation, marketing, management, and ownership of Web-based sex businesses. In the words of Danni Ashe, the world's most downloaded woman according to the *Guinness Book of Records*, "the power structure is changing . . . the performers are more involved. Virtually every woman in the business now has her own site."

The industry is expanding, adopting standard business practices, consolidating, and striving to achieve a degree of legitimacy (and thereby access to larger markets). One or two companies have successfully floated on the stock market; others have tried, or are exploring the options. For example, Private Media, a Barcelona-based supplier of hardcore pornography, already has a listing on the NAS-DAQ and is exploring the possibility of a European stock market listing. Of course, there is still a high level of resistance among the financial and banking establishment: pornography may not be difficult to sell on the Web, but it may be difficult to sell the idea of representing porn merchants to one's traditional blue chip clients. That said, when *Playboy Enterprises* announced that it was abandoning its soft-porn-only policy and moving into hardcore distribution, its stock price rose by 12 percent. Money talks, the moral majority notwithstanding!

This explosion of consumer interest is not hard to understand. Eros and technology have always gone hand in hand. In modern times, the VCR had a liberating effect on pent-up consumer demand for pornography, as did the plain ol' telephone (Americans spend hundreds of millions annually on phone sex), so we perhaps shouldn't be surprised that the Internet and World Wide Web are facilitating new modes of providing and consuming pornographic goods, and also creating new environments (chat rooms, Web rings) and novel experiences (public voyeurism, interactive sex) for the insatiable consumer.

The extraordinary demand for online sexual titillation, coupled with intense competition among commercial sex sites, has meant that the (much stigmatized) adult entertainment industry has been at the cutting edge of technology. In the words of a Sun Microsystems spokesperson, "The way you know if your technology is good is if it's doing well in the porn world." E-commerce innovations to have come out of the adult entertainment sector include banner advertising, partnership programs/syndicates, and outsourcing, along with less appealing practices such as search engine manipulation and pop-up windows. More specifically, the structural dynamics of the adult entertainment business itself are changing, and not a few orthodoxies and stereotypes are being challenged by recent trends. For scholars, the ongoing transformation of the adult entertainment industry affords an intriguing opportunity to study the mutual shaping of technology and human values. For librarians, the lid is about to be blown off Pandora's box.

REFERENCE

Cronin, B., and E. Davenport. "E-rogenous Zones: Positioning Pornography in the Digital Economy." *The Information Society* 17, no. 1 (2001): 33–48.

Whatever Happened to Common Sense?

Originally published September 2000

"Hardware-store owners are not professionals; librarians believe that they are." The quote comes from an illuminating but, sadly, little cited, study by Lawrence White, entitled *The Public Library in the 1980s*. (White, by the way, was an economist.) I was reminded of it recently when reading the 1998 NCLIS (National Commission on Libraries and Information Science) report *Kids and the Internet: The Promise and the Perils*. For many librarians, professionalism is most tellingly exercised in the ways they select and provide materials for public use. Professional librarians decide, on the public's behalf, what kinds of materials will be made available. I presume it is this that, more than anything else, distinguishes them from the typical hardware store owner, who merely provides his customers with what they want. Most public librarians, judging by what I read in the pages of *LJ* and *American Libraries*, seem to have an implacable antipathy to filtering or censorship of any kind: this despite the fact that selection, the defining professional skill, necessarily entails such. Increasingly, prolix policies and grandiloquent tracts—think of the *Library Bill of Rights*—are used to create the trappings of moral and legal certitude around the dominant view that any form of censorship is unacceptable.

This absolutism reveals itself in the NCLIS report. Ms. Symons, the then-president of the ALA (American Library Association), reminds us in her testimony that the organization's policy is "one against filtering." That policy appears to oppose denying or filtering children's access to websites and chat rooms where obscene images and discussion of child pornography can be expected. Now, hardware store owners don't usually let kids play with, or purchase, chain saws. The law would not smile favorably on such behavior and, in any case, common sense tells us that such a laissez-faire attitude to child rearing would be morally myopic. But, apparently, common sense has no place in the postmodern library. This observation is confirmed by the opening testimony of Andrew Vachss, an attorney, novelist, and life-long library advocate. Let me quote a few lines from his powerful remarks to the NCLIS hearing: "You know what the greatest threat to vulnerable children is? It is the very real potential for enticement. Child pornography has always existed. Predatory pedophiles have always lurked outside playgrounds and inside organizations. But the Internet permits, in its interactive form, access to children that would not be available to them otherwise." If you're in any way skeptical, I suggest you pick up a copy of Katherine Tarbox's *Katie.com*, a thirteen-year-old's account of her online seduction by a forty-one-year-old pedophile.

Vachss acknowledges the broad educational value of the Internet, and focuses his remarks on interactive environments where predators can prey with relative ease. Let me quote again: "As a research tool, I think the Internet has much to offer. But 'chat' is not research. And while it is most certainly a form of 'speech,' the enticement of children for the sexual gratification of an adult is not a protected form of speech." Commonsensical, you might think, but apparently not as far as the vast majority of the ALA's Council is concerned. Here, the protection of minors takes a back seat to the protection of self-image. But, unfortunately, there is a gap between the idealized self-image and actuality. According to Ms. Symons, all but two of the ALA's 170 council members voted against filtering. Elsewhere in the NCLIS report, it was noted that approximately 15 percent of U.S. public libraries employ filtering. So, some of those who voted against filtering very likely work in libraries that use filtering!

I concede that this is a hideously complicated topic in which constitutional law, professional values, state mandates, parental rights, and community standards collide. But I would have hoped that common sense might guide us through the Charybdis of illegality and the Scylla of social irresponsibility. Common sense tells us that shouting "fire" in a crowded theater is not an acceptable thing to do; common sense also tells us that facilitating children's access to potentially harmful materials (illegal obscenity) and persons (child pornographers) is dumb. This is not an occasion for what Mr. Vachss termed "sloganeering." We are *not* debating the pros and cons of pornography, but postulating that a civilized society can, and should, take steps to minimize identifiable threats posed to minors by deviants. Give me an iota of common sense rather than a 300-page manual on intellectual freedom.

Imagine a child searching the Web in a library to find information for a school project. I recently (May 4, 2000) used a number of seemingly innocuous search terms on a well-known Web search engine (Excite) to find out what proportion of the returned URLs linked to pornographic websites. In each case below, I give the proportion of the top-ten matches pointing to porn sites (these, in turn, may link to other sex sites and chat rooms): "animals" = 7/10; "ass" = 10/10; "farmyard" = 1/10; "body" = 7/10; "girls" = 9/10; "boys" = 8/10. A child entering the term "animals" is more likely to find a site dealing with bestiality rather than with pets or zoos. "Ass" turns up no donkeys, but links to a variety of hard-core porn sites. Searching for "farmyard," the same child will find at least one site dealing with bestiality, tucked between two others offering sliding-block puzzles for kids. This, of course, is only the start of the slippery slope so graphically described by Mr. Vachss.

Why is it that some public libraries don't stock *Playboy* or *Penthouse* (or, if they do, keep them behind the shelves) but will allow users, including, in some cases, children, to access the websites of the parallel cyberbusinesses created by Messrs. Hefner and Guccione? What is the justification for excluding, or secreting, printed pornography (soft or otherwise) while facilitating access to a digital pornocopia—to use Laurence O'Toole's coinage? Why does collection development begin at the library door but end at the computer screen? Children's librarians select the materials that my kids borrow weekly from the public library, but for some reason they seem reluctant to apply the same principles to the world of online resources. Logically, there's no reason not to apply content selection to the Web. For instance, OCLC (Online Computer Library Center) and some 150 member-libraries are actively engaged in the CORC (Cooperative Online Resource Catalog) project to develop a database of reliable, Web-based resources, while Apple's KidSafe is protection software that allows access only to sites determined by professional teachers to have educational value. Why couldn't children's librarians do something similar, either locally or collaboratively? Hiding behind the pages of the *Intellectual Freedom Manual* (ALA 1996, 5th ed.) won't do. The choice is simple: be a *professional* librarian or go work in a hardware store.

REFERENCES

Tarbox, K. *Katie.com.* New York: Dutton, 2000.

U.S. Commission on Libraries and Information Science. *Kids and the Internet: The Promise and the Perils.* Washington, D.C.: NCLIS, 1998.

White, L. *The Public Library in the 1980s.* Lexington, Mass: Lexington Books, 1983.

COMMON NONSENSE

Common sense may not be so uncommon, after all. That's my conclusion based on the tenor of the feedback I received in the wake of "Whatever Happened to Common Sense?" By way of illustration, one academic library director congratulated me on my "concise and sensible observations," a couple of (librarian) mothers of young children expressed their gratitude at my raising a position that they felt had been denied an adequate hearing, and another professional librarian (in a letter published in *LJ*) highlighted "the blinded approach by our professional association" to the question of children and the availability of Web-based pornography in libraries. Others, including some of our own students at Indiana University, were less than happy with the relativism of my stance. The issues raised in this piece typically have a dramatically polarizing effect on professional discourse, as we have seen over the years.

The debate that swirls around "hot button" topics like filtering throws into relief the inherent contradictions of this country. The battle lines between libertarians and fundamentalists on the question of pornography and censorship are inescapably obvious to one and all. And the war of words is unrelenting, with legions of lawyers and lobbyists lined up on both sides. It's quite a spectacle for those of us from distant shores; rather edifying, yet sad in a way, as the debate, ultimately, seems to go nowhere. Moreover, one is struck by the absence of middle ground, the traditional home of common sense.

Of course, it's singularly unfashionable within our professional world to suggest that there may, on occasion, be grounds for imposing restrictions on the resources provided by publicly funded institutions such as libraries, even when we are talking about materials that are technically in breach of federal law and potentially harmful to minors. As Neil Postman (1999, 134) said in a slightly different context, "civil libertarians fear the erosion of speech more than they fear the erosion of childhood." However well-intentioned a proposal, it inevitably falls at the altar of absolutism: "Thou shalt not censor" is the unyielding and self-righteous response from those for whom the First Amendment must be interpreted literally. The current live issue is the Children's Internet Protection Act (CIPA), which went into effect in spring of 2001. These laws place restrictions on the use of funding that is available through the Library Services and Technology Act, Title III of the Elementary and Secondary Education Act, and on the Universal Service discount program known as the E-rate. The restrictions take the form of requirements for Internet safety policies and technology that would block or filter certain material on the Internet from being accessed via a computer running the blocking software. Predictably, the executive board of the American Library Association is not well pleased about having the legislative branch of government step on its sacred turf, and duly initiated a legal challenge against the CIPA with (again) the support of the ACLU (American Civil Liberties Union).

At this point, I should declare an interest: I worked as a consultant/expert witness with the U.S. Department of Justice on the CIPA, and thus it may be felt that I have a particular ax to grind. However, for the record, I agreed to lend my services to the government's case not because of any moral or ideological views I might hold in respect of the subject—give me Nadine Strossen (1996) over Catherine MacKinnon or Andrea Dworkin any day of the week—but because of the manifest hypocrisy of the ALA's position. We all know that sexually explicit materials are noticeable by their absence from the shelves of public libraries. Even that American icon *Playboy* is something of a rarity in the nation's libraries, and where it is to be found, you'll likely have to make a special request to get your hands on it. Pornography is effectively invisible in American libraries not because Americans don't like pornography—many clearly do—but because most librarians don't like the idea of having pornography in their collections. As Bill Katz (1971, 4061) noted three decades ago: "the avoidance of *Playboy* in many libraries is an expression of the librarian's confidence that he knows what is best for B, all six million of the Bs who read the magazine everywhere but in the library." For better or worse, America's public libraries are not, and never have been, repositories of pornographic materials. The ALA, however, willfully ignores this fact in its holier-than-thou refusal to condone the filtering of obscene material accessible via the Web, yet librarians, for whatever admixture of reasons, have consistently denied pornography a place in their collections. Indeed, even John Berry III, that unwavering opponent of censorship, recently had the good grace to acknowledge in one of his *LJ* editorials "the growing distance between the ALA's positions and library practice" (Berry 2002, 8).

On the one hand, I wonder what proportion of the ALA's membership, whose dues presumably partly pay for the organization's expensive team of lawyers and expert witnesses, endorses the challenge to the Children's Internet Protection Act. And, on the other, I'd like to know how many U.S. citizens—parents, in particular—are comfortable with the idea of their tax dollars being used to underwrite the electronic provision of potentially illegal materials in public spaces. What a shame that "First Amendment pietism," to appropriate Henry Louis Gates' (1992, 898) term, trumps common sense in East Huron Street!

REFERENCES

Berry, J. N. "Editorial—Fear of Information." *Library Journal* (April 15, 2002): 8.

Gates, H. L. "To Deprave and Corrupt." *The Nation* (June 29, 1992): 898–903.

Katz, B. "The Pornography Collection." *Library Journal* (December 15, 1971): 4060–66.

Postman, N. *Building a Bridge to the 18th Century: How the Past Can Improve Our Future*. New York: Vintage Books, 1999.

Strossen, N. *Defending Pornography: Free Speech, Sex, and the Fight for Women's Rights*. New York: Anchor, 1996.

Selection and Censorship: Splitting Hairs

Censorship is a dirty word within the library world. The American Library Association (ALA) is certainly not coy about highlighting attempts by individuals or groups to censor library materials. Its website lists the 100 most frequently banned books for 1990–2000 and also provides information on Banned Books Week (www.ala.org/bbooks /top100bannedbooks.html). By way of contrast, the organization is intriguingly silent on the matter of covert censorship as practiced by librarians. One man's censorship is another man's selection, I suppose.

Selection and censorship have a reciprocal relationship. The net effect of an item not being added to a library collection (i.e., selected) is no different from its being consciously excluded by a librarian (i.e., censored), as far as the patron or author is concerned. To argue otherwise is simply disingenuous, no disrespect to the late Lester Asheim (1953), author of the oft-quoted paper "Not Censorship but Selection." That, of course, is not to say that every item that is not selected has been censored, since most libraries can afford to purchase (and store) only a fraction of what is published. However, there is a gray zone between what might be termed active and passive censorship that both Asheim and some others in the profession seem rather reluctant to acknowledge, and it is in this penumbral zone that covert or "subterranean" censorship (a term coined by Morris Ernst and quoted in Asheim above) is exercised.

The ALA has copious guidelines for creating and implementing selection policies within school media centers and public libraries (www.ala.org/alaorg/oif/workbook_selection.html#objectives). Its website also includes sample polices along with exhaustive criteria for selecting library materials. Well intentioned though such resource materials may be, they, naturally, cannot ensure that an individual's preferences, cultural biases, and unconscious prejudices do not play some role in the selection process, a point tellingly, if for the ALA inconveniently, documented by Marjorie Fiske (1968, 65–66). Her highly revealing survey of book selection practices in both public and school libraries uncovered a significant discrepancy between theory and practice. It is worth quoting her findings:

> When it comes to actual practice, nearly two thirds of all librarians who have a say in book selection reported instances where the controversiality of a book or an author resulted in a decision not to buy. Nearly one fifth habitually avoid buying any material which is known to be controversial. . . . It is doubtful whether many librarians would agree that consistency is always a virtue in book selection, but it is also doubtful whether many are quite aware of the extent of their inconsistencies in buying controversial books.

Before you dismiss these otherwise compelling findings as dated and thus of limited value, let me fast-forward to the 1990s and a study carried out by Leigh Estabrook and Chris Horak (1992, 53) that nicely reinforced Fiske's conclusions. In their survey of both public library users and library personnel, they found, inter alia, that only 30 percent of librarians thought *Playboy* and *Penthouse* magazines should be available to everyone, while 37 percent of librarians said that such magazines should not be in libraries at all. (Library patrons were even less tolerant of such materials, it should be noted.) These observations and views don't sit comfortably with the ALA's high-minded public pronouncements on the topics of censorship and selection. Indeed, the ALA blimpishly refuses to admit what we all know to be the case: American public libraries do not and never have collected pornography. (If human sexuality and its representation is your thing, you'll just have to come to Indiana University Bloomington, home to the world-renowned Kinsey Institute and its marvelous collections of print materials, artifacts, and art work [www.indiana .edu/~kinsey/].) The problem, of course, is that many mainstream Americans have an avid interest in pornography, an interest that is simply not reflected in the collections of the nation's public libraries. When it comes to philately or numismatics, of course, it's a very different story: the shelves will be generously stocked with books and magazines devoted to stamps and coins. But *amateurs* of pornography and erotica are shortchanged. The facts speak for themselves, but the ALA priggishly ignores the glaring inconsistencies in professional practice, resorting to Orwellian Newspeak.

Nothing new in any of this, for as Bill Katz (1971, 4061) noted in the seventies, "Selection . . . consists of avoiding the thorny thicket of sex." Yet, the ALA seems utterly impervious to the gulf between the rhetoric of the *Library Bill of Rights*, which notes that librarians "have a public and professional obligation to provide equal access to all library resources for all library users" (see www.ala.org/alaorg /oif/acc_chil.html), and the material reality of contemporary library practice. The issue is not whether public libraries should or shouldn't stock pornography (that's a topic for another day . . . and another author perhaps) but why the ALA is incapable of acknowl-edging the fact that subterranean censorship is routinely practiced within the profession. The organization's public stance on the mat-ter of censorship is at best inconsistent and at worst hypocritical. More to the point, it's hopelessly at odds with the values of the ma-jority of its card-carrying members. Regrettably, the bureaucratic tail seems to be wagging the professional dog.

REFERENCES

Asheim, L. "Not Censorship but Selection." *Wilson Library Bulletin* 28 (1953): 63–67.

Estabrook, L., and C. Horack. "Public vs. Professional Opinion on Libraries: The Great Divide." *Library Journal* 117, no. 6 (1992): 52–55.

Fiske, M. *Book Selection and Censorship: A Study of School and Public Libraries in California*. Berkeley: University of California Press, 1968.

Katz, B. "The Pornography Collection." *Library Journal* (December 15, 1971): 4060–66.

CUSTOMER SATISFACTION

Originally published October 2000

"Medical mistakes a leading cause of death." The headline-grabbing claim is all too familiar, but no less distressing. In the United States, medical error allegedly causes more deaths than cancer or heart attacks. Doctors, nurses, and other health care practitioners may be highly educated, professionally certified, and technologically sophisticated, but they still make mistakes. Iatrogenic dysfunction writ large. In medicine, as in other less critical walks of life such as librarianship, certification and accreditation do not add up to infallibility. But we already know that. Remember the "55 Percent Rule"—the old canard that reference librarians get the answer wrong almost half the time? I have not heard much lately about "half right services," Hernon and McClure's apt phrase from an earlier *LJ* (April 15, 1986), but I can still remember struggling to reconcile pious proclamations of professionalism with embarrassing levels of incorrect information provision.

Of course, getting the height of the Eiffel Tower wrong is not exactly life critical, but, cumulatively, such bloopers can have a corrosive effect upon public perceptions of professional competence. If the graduate output of professionally accredited library and information science programs can get it wrong so consistently and so often, what's the value of accreditation? Specifically, what assurances does accreditation offer the public at large about the professional competence of those being hired to staff libraries? It seems not unreasonable to conclude that accreditation per se is no guarantee of acceptable service quality. So, from the public's perspective we might as well ditch accreditation, which is, after all, an input measure, and shift the focus to quality of service delivered—an output measure.

Wearing my consumer hat, I'm typically more interested in what comes out than what goes in. Do I really care if the chef at my favorite restaurant studied under Marco Pierre White and has a

Michelin star, if what is served up is bereft of culinary imagination and the service sullen? Look at it from another angle: my local newspaper occasionally publishes the results of restaurant inspections. I'm indebted to it for alerting me to substandard public health safety provision and, I like to think, for shaming those who should know better into doing better. When it comes to eating, we're obsessive about service and standards. Not so with libraries.

All of which leads to the inevitable question, why don't we have local, state, or national standards for libraries? Why don't we gather and publicize meaningful performance measures, as we do for restaurants—and just about everything else? Why don't we encourage benchmarking, if, as Pirsig put it memorably in *Zen and the Art of Motorcycle Maintenance*, "quality is the track which drives the train"? Standard setting is not exactly a novel idea. Thomas Hennen outlined a wide variety of approaches in the March 2000 issue of *America Libraries*. I am not, however, advocating a return to the prescriptive standards of the 1970s and 1980s—remember the 1973 IFLA *Standards for Public Libraries*? Nor am I advocating that we exhume the ALA's *Output Measures for Public Libraries*. Frankly, I'm more interested in the actual than the aspirational; concrete consumer satisfaction indicators, in other words. Among the proposals suggested by Hennen are applying the ISO 9000 quality management standard to libraries, and testing libraries using a customer satisfaction index, such as the ACSI (American Customer Satisfaction Index). If HMOs and hotels can conduct regular customer satisfaction surveys, perhaps the library community should think about instituting the practice.

Some years ago, I was part of the team commissioned by the United Kingdom government's Department of National Heritage to undertake a large-scale survey of public library provision and use, and make recommendations for the future development of libraries. The resultant report, *Review of the Public Library Service in England and Wales*, highlighted, inter alia, the divergent perceptions of the public and the library profession. In brief, they didn't see us as we saw ourselves. The Benton Foundation's 1996 study of the role of libraries in the digital age, *Buildings, Books, and Bytes*, drew similar conclusions. This dissonance is symptomatic of what is awry in our field. A "we know better than you" approach just won't fly these days. Infantilizing users is not exactly a killer customer relationship-building strategy.

In the United Kingdom, central government's mania for public accountability, embodied in something called Best Value Performance

Indicators (BVPIs), has percolated to the public library sector. Among the battery of BVPIs currently in use, three relate specifically to library services: cost per visit, total visits, percentage of users who found or reserved what they wanted. The third of these, once it is tweaked to take account of virtual visits, may get close to the kind of measures I have in mind. At least, it's a well-intentioned start. In addition to the aforementioned BVPIs, the U.K. Audit Commission has also set up an independent inspection service for local authorities, which includes at least one library-related indicator. And if that weren't enough, the Department for Culture, Media & Sport, the government body responsible for libraries, requires library authorities in England and Wales to submit Annual Library Plans for appraisal. These plans are expected to address broad issues, such as the role of the public library in combating social exclusion. They are then graded (poor, satisfactory, good) and made publicly available. All of this is very British (and somewhat aspirational), but it does suggest that accountability is beginning to catch on at the grassroots level. A sign of the times, no doubt.

Another sign of the times was the media attention showered on Malcom McLaren, the man who brought us the Sex Pistols. McLaren recently ran as an independent candidate to be mayor of London. One of his most-quoted proposals was to introduce pubs into London's public libraries. The logic was simple: if the revenue from the sale of alcohol were used to buy more new books, library use would increase. The concept of Andrew Carnegie's joint use libraries, with their public baths, billiard rooms, etc., might just have experienced a renaissance as a result of an erstwhile punk rock star's belief that customer care mattered. Cheers, Malcolm, for reminding us in roundabout fashion that accreditation and quality of service are not one and the same!

REFERENCES

Aslib. *Review of the Public Library Service in England and Wales for the Department of National Heritage.* London: Aslib, 1995.

Benton Foundation. *Buildings, Books, and Bytes: Libraries and Communities in the Digital Age.* Washington, D.C.: Benton Foundation, 1996.

Hennen, T. J. "Why We Should Establish a National System of Standards." *American Libraries* 31, no. 3 (2000): 43–45.

Hernon, P., and C. McClure. "Unobtrusive Reference Testing: The 55 Percent Rule." *LJ* (April 15, 1986): 37–41.

Rank Injustice?

Originally published November 2000

Lies, damned lies, and statistics. Looking at yet another set of program rankings brought Mark Twain's words to mind. We certainly have a mania for counting and ranking—did you know that Indiana University Bloomington ranks among the top ten in terms of the attractiveness of its campus, or that our music librarianship program ranks #1 in the nation? (I'm duty bound to point out that only one other school featured in the latter category.) Annual rankings of universities, such as those produced by *U.S. News & World Report*, are eagerly awaited by prospective students, parents, and the professorate. The same is true of *Business Week*'s rankings of MBA programs, and increasingly for other subject-specific surveys. Who knows where it will all end? A few months ago, the *Chronicle of Higher Education* ran a story on dotcom (and other) millionaires in faculty ranks, noting that a third of Stanford University's computer science faculty already had millionaire status. How soon before we see departments ranked in terms of their faculty's net worth?

Measurement mania has caught on elsewhere. In the United Kingdom, the government gathers masses of quantitative and qualitative data every four or five years in order to rank universities in terms of their research output. The Research Assessment Exercise (RAE) covers virtually every subject area in every university. This is no mere beauty competition; results from the RAE directly and materially affect research funding levels in individual departments. These are rankings with teeth, and several countries are starting to take note.

Other rankings, however, seem to be little more than pretexts for preening. The annual publication of the ARL (Association of Research Libraries) library statistics in the *Chronicle of Higher Education* has library deans and directors scrambling to issue press releases— or not, as the case may be. But remember what's being measured:

collection size, annual acquisition levels, and overall library spending. Small may be beautiful, as Schumacher said, but big is better still. Don't get me wrong: I'm thrilled to be at an institution that has top-flight library collections, but I sometimes wonder if massification is a meaningful measure in the age of the virtual digital library. At what point will we acknowledge our own professional rhetoric by evaluating institutions in terms of their ability to provide users with access to remote collections rather than the size of their local holdings?

Universities are now being ranked in terms of their "wiredness." This year, *Yahoo! Internet Life* magazine's survey placed Indiana University Bloomington fourth overall in the nation on a battery of measures, including computer availability, e-mail usage and access, Web space usage, networking, and Web-related courses. Naturally, I'm happy to trumpet the fact in our promotional literature, without actually pointing out that quite a few prestigious schools (Harvard, Yale) and a number of public universities with lots of "Big Iron" (Michigan, Berkeley) declined to participate. These schools took exception to the fact that *Yahoo!* refuses to divulge its scoring formula, a not uncommon reaction, and one with which Jack Gourman, author of the eponymous *Report*, is all too familiar. I checked the latest (i.e., 1997) Gourman Report to see what the author says about the bases for his graduate program rankings, but could find no description whatsoever of the method used. I may feel good that Indiana ranks #3 in his survey of library science schools, but I'd feel a lot better if I had some idea of the grounds for his assessment. Indiana got a score of 4.86 out of a possible 5; precise, to be sure, but close to meaningless, I suspect.

A few years ago, *U.S. News & World Report* decided to include library science (on a biennial basis) in its high-profile rankings. I was one of those randomly selected to be a respondent in the first survey, which, to be blunt, would not have passed muster in Survey Research 101. Basically, we were asked to score other institutions on a simple rating scale. A few faculty responded from each school, and the scores were totted up to yield a quality indicator (at least, that's what I think happened). In essence, the *U.S. News & World Report* survey is not all that different from the perception studies my predecessor Herb White used to publish in *LQ*, but it's got much more cachet. Most of us with decent rankings have the *U.S. News & World Report* logo emblazoned on our Web pages, flagging the fact that we're, if not quite best of breed, at least of solid pedigree. Mischievously, I might observe that the University of North Carolina at Chapel Hill boasts of being "ranked #1" while the University of Illinois at Urbana-Champaign, with which it actually tied for top slot, merely provides a link to the original story. I'm not being critical of UNC (I'd do exactly the same), merely noting subtle differences in approaches to boosterism among our peer institutions.

If the truth be told, we are selectively blind to the design limitations of the surveys we so readily invoke to promote our schools. We wouldn't tolerate such shoddy work from our students, and would lampoon our peers if their published research were based on such methodologically shaky foundations. All of this would matter, if it mattered. But it doesn't, for the very simple reason that there's considerable agreement between the various studies. That is to say, the population of top-ranking schools is pretty consistent from one survey to the next, though there is intensified jostling for pole position. I'll happily concede that Michigan, Illinois, and North Carolina are all good schools but, naturally, I'm reluctant to concede that they are better than Indiana, which our #6 ranking in the *U.S. News & World Report* might seem to imply. I'm even more reluctant to grant any such concession in the light of a recent six-year quantitative study of LIS schools' scholarly production and impact, published in *LQ* (April 2000). John Budd's detailed study rates and weights each program on a range of measures, from which he creates a composite score. He then compares the rankings derived from his composite scores with those of the latest *U.S. News & World Report* perception study. Thanks to Budd, the ugly ducking that was Indiana is magically transformed into a #1 ranking swan. Moral of the story? Shop around until you find a ranking that fits.

FOR WHOM THE BELL CURVE TOLLS

Originally published January 2001

"And the second runner-up is . . ." Once upon a time there was a winner and a runner-up. Life was simple. Language had meaning. Today, we have runners-up to the power of n, whether it's the Miss America pageant or the local agricultural fair. That way, no one's feelings get hurt. I first noticed the trend nine years ago at the Monroe County Fair, where all pies in the apple pie competition had received splendid rosettes. Even the most desiccated and malformed specimen warranted formal recognition. Bathing beauties or baked beauties, everyone is a winner in today's "feel-good" world. We're applauded for taking part, for expressing a view, for being inadequate, and for failing. Mere participation, in our postmodern culture, merits a prize.

It's pretty much the same in academia. We call it grade inflation. Students are crestfallen if awarded anything lower than a B+ for their course work, despite the fact that B+ equates with "very good." But being "very good" is not good enough, if you've been raised on a diet of As and the attendant belief that anything less is tantamount to failure. So, rather than deal with suicidal students and vague threats of litigation, we delude ourselves with the comforting thought that Lake Wobegon can be replicated across the nation's campuses. We're all excellent, and the bell curve be damned! But there is a knock-on effect: bright students are clamoring for the introduction of a new grade, A++, to distinguish real merit from feel-good merit. The corrosive effect of this trend came home to me forcibly when my son announced proudly that he had (at elementary school) scored 103 on a test with a maximum (i.e., perfect) score of 100. We're launched on an inflationary spiral that insults common sense, but is designed to make us feel good about ourselves. For an excoriating analysis of academe's ills in this regard, I recommend Bill Readings' *The University in Ruins* (1996).

The malaise manifests itself in many ways. Step into the typical professional office (dentist, accountant, professor) and what do you see? Plaques. A profusion of plaques—on walls, desktops, and shelves. Framed copies of degrees, certificates, testimonials, and countless other forms of recognition by one's peers and the community at large are everywhere to be seen. It's a national disease. Frankly, it's hard to know whether we are reassuring ourselves or our clients. Who feels better, them or us?

Take our own field. Each of our professional associations has a battery of annual and other awards. Go to the ALISE (Association for Library and Information Science Education) home page and you'll find a list, including annual awards for service, teaching, and innovation. Stay in the organization for a couple of decades, don't blot your copybook, and by the law of averages you could end up getting a gong (the ALISE membership is only about 600). On the ASIS (American Society for Information Science) web page, you'll find a list of twenty-one awards, including the "chapter event of the year." The trick here is to get yourself elected local chapter chair, throw a fabulous party to which you'll invite the incumbent president, and, bingo, a gong could be yours for the asking (not that you'll ask, of course). When we turn to the ALA's (American Library Association) home page, it's clear that we have moved into the big league. There are literally hundreds of awards, prizes, citations, professional achievement awards, and named scholarships. Pay your dues, stay sober, and keep your hand out of the till should probably be enough to make you eligible for some kind of ALA award before the sun sets on your career.

I don't mean to deprecate those who have received awards (after all, I've got a couple of tiny, silver-plated salvers to show for my efforts over the years), but the proliferation of honors creates a variant of Gresham's Law: trivial awards drive serious accomplishments out of sight. I read scores, if not hundreds, of CVs each year, but am utterly bamboozled by the seemingly infinite number of achievement awards available in our spheres of concern. The net effect is that I ignore most of them, unless I happen to spot one that has some real pedigree and substance to it. It's worth remembering that talent, motivation, and commitment are not distributed equally. In all walks of life, a relatively few individuals make a significant difference. That's why, historically, we have had a system of honors (Nobel laureates, the Victoria Cross, Olympic medals) that acknowledges genuinely superior achievement in a variety of contexts. The commodification of awards merely diminishes the prevailing currency and calls into disrepute the whole process of bestowing public honors and recognition. Prevailing practice in the United States is now as unseemly and absurd, in its own way, as the British system of political honors, preferments, and "plumage positions" so brilliantly evoked by David Cannadine (1999).

Lamentably, one also sees a marked decline in university standards—even at reputable institutions. In recent years, the number of honorary doctorates awarded to nonscholars (rock stars, entrepreneurs, media celebrities) has risen appreciably. In Britain, some of the new universities dish out doctorates as if they were going out of fashion. Recipients may be worthy individuals, but their connections and contributions to academia are tenuous, at best. All too often, the honorific is in return for (or, worse, the expectation of) a benefaction of some kind. Gongs for greenbacks, not to put too fine a point on it (Cronin 2002). I do, of course, understand the reasons for this less than salubrious practice, but perhaps a new kind of institutional award could be created for those whose contributions do not fall within the scholarly realm. That way, the cachet of an honorary doctorate might just be preserved without the dispensing institutions having to forego future endowment income.

It's time to acknowledge that we can't all be excellent. Most of us will make worthy professional contributions over the course of our careers. And that is as it should be. But being worthy is insufficient grounds for public recognition. It is time to cull the nominating committees, put away the plaques, and concentrate on the substance of the job. Let distinction announce itself.

REFERENCES

Cannadine, D. *The Decline and Fall of the British Aristocracy.* New York: Vintage Books, 1999.

Cronin, B. Honoris Causa, forthcoming.

Readings, B. *The University in Ruins.* Cambridge, Mass.: Harvard University Press, 1996.

You may be interested to know that a Harvard professor has launched a campaign against grade inflation by giving students in his political science course two grades: one for the registrar and the public record, the other in private. Needless to say, not everyone sees the funny side of this tactic (see http://chronicle.com/free/v47/i30/30b0241.htm).

THE MOTHER OF ALL MYTHS

Originally published February 2001

I cringe every time I hear the dreaded words *library faculty status*. For almost a decade, I've watched firsthand as otherwise sensible and professionally responsible colleagues engage in the folderol of faculty governance. My librarian colleagues, that is. Faculty governance as exercised by faculty (a.k.a. the professorate) is quite a different matter. That I understand and, despite the occasional frustrations (from an administrator's perspective) of the self-governance model, I can readily appreciate the social benefits of a system that seeks to protect academic freedom and curricular integrity. Having watched Margaret Thatcher extirpate tenure from the United Kingdom higher education system during her prime ministership, I am all the more appreciative of the personal and institutional benefits afforded by this much maligned, seemingly anachronistic, but ultimately enlightened, practice. However, tenure and the paraphernalia of the academic calling have nothing whatsoever to do with the praxis of librarianship.

It's more than fifty years since the University of Illinois became the first major academic institution to grant faculty status to librarians. Today, it's estimated that approximately half of all librarians in the U.S. higher education sector have faculty status. Since the rot set in at Illinois, innumerable journal articles and opinion pieces have been published on the subject of faculty status for librarians. All in all, it makes for depressing reading. The lack of logic, limpness of argument, and blatant grasping for status signifiers revealed in much of this literature are breathtaking. Some of the justifications are not just silly, but downright embarrassing. Faculty status, we're told, means that librarians interact more confidently with the mainstream faculty, use more analytic approaches to the management of library services, and bring fresh perspectives to bear on their work through research and participation in national associations.

Two immediate responses to these, and similar, claims suggest themselves: first, where is the evidence, and, second, why in heaven's name would having faculty status necessarily result in any of these outcomes? Not surprisingly, those who have actually poked behind the inflated rhetoric find that the evidence is wanting. Bruce Kingma and Gillian McCombs, for example, looked at the opportunity cost of faculty status for libraries and found some interesting, not to say counterintuitive, results. Using a battery of measures on ARL (Association of Research Libraries) member institutions, they discovered that professional productivity and faculty status were negatively correlated. To put it simply, you get less for more as a result of conferring faculty status on professional librarians; or, in their more diplomatic words, "faculty status for librarians is not cost neutral." I recall a senior administrator's (perhaps tongue-in-cheek) comment to the effect that his institution granted tenure to librarians because that way they could be paid less. Of course, that's a rather myopic and simplistic form of accounting. The lifetime opportunity cost of even a few immobile and underperforming (tenured) librarians is nontrivial, and could easily exceed the presumptive salary savings.

Over the years, I've interacted with scores of professional librarians, but I could not for the life of me distinguish those with faculty status from those beyond the pale. I've also interacted with librarians before and after they've achieved tenure and/or been promoted, and I can't say that I've noticed any cognitive, behavioral, or affective amelioration as a result. Good librarians are good librarians, with or without faculty status. Some are scholars manqués and publish in their marginal time. And that is to be commended. Others teach, and schools such as my own depend on regular input from such committed colleagues. But universities don't confer faculty status on the many others (from industry, the professions and the local community) who teach for them on an adjunct basis, so why should librarians be granted preferential status?

Wrapping the mantle of faculty status around oneself makes not the slightest difference as far as the user is concerned, but it does on occasion invite the quiet mockery of the professorate. If you don't believe me, I suggest you take a look at a typical dossier for a librarian seeking promotion and tenure at a major research university. Talk about contrivance and misallocation of effort! It's an egregious case of square pegs in round holes. To add insult to injury, the whole process consumes considerable institutional resources. If all the time spent writing often forgettable articles for journals of often questionable quality and compiling bloated dossiers were converted into service delivery, we'd all be much better off—as, indeed, would our institutions' library acquisitions budgets.

Indiana University is blessed with a wonderful library and some first-rate librarians, factors that, here as elsewhere, can play a part in recruiting and retaining faculty. That said, I am astonished at the fervor with which more than a few of my colleagues (and, again, this is by no means a local phenomenon) are wedded to the idea of faculty status. Worse, I am dismayed at the amount of time and energy they deflect from their primary professional duties and channel into interminable meetings on the arcana of faculty governance. Worse still, it appears that our librarian colleagues' enthusiasm for faculty governance is greater than that of the bona fide faculty, judging by the proportional representation data that I've seen locally. Ah, the righteous zeal of the newly converted!

To an outsider, it all seems so petty and vainglorious, and, for once, I'm forced to side with my old sparring partner, Herb White. White, in dismissing the holy grail of faculty status, makes the point that no right-thinking individual would assume that "a large, high-quality library and a large staff of high-quality librarians are independent variables." In other words, do a good job and the results will speak for themselves. Faculty status, whatever the feel-good factor, won't compensate for mediocre professional skills, nor materially improve the application of already honed skills. If anything, the obsession with status merely detracts from customer service and weakens the profession's public image. Librarians, along with information systems specialists and sundry other members of the campus community, are professional employees whose role is to support, not define or negotiate, the academic mission of the university. Fifty years of conceit is probably enough.

REFERENCES

Kingma, B., and G. McCombs. "The Opportunity Costs of Faculty Status for Academic Librarians." *College & Research Libraries* 56 (1995): 258–64.

White, H. S. "Faculty Status for Academic Librarians: The Search for the Holy Grail." *Library Journal* (November 15, 1996): 40.

MYTHING THE POINT

The "Mother of All Myths" article produced the mother of all mailbags. It may also have provoked, in part, Shannon Cary's article, "Faculty Rank, Status, and Tenure." This short overview provides helpful information regarding the number of institutions granting tenure, faculty-equivalent salaries, and other privileges to academic librarians. According to Cary's classification, full tenure is awarded by 44 percent of institutions, partial by 21 percent, and none by 35 percent. Full salary equivalence is provided in 39 percent of cases. She concludes, "Regardless of the controversy over the role of librarians in the academic community, it is clear that many librarians are receiving the rights and responsibilities of faculty status." It may well be the case that the rot has set in more deeply than I had imagined, but at least a healthy number of institutions has managed to resist this unnecessary and insidious trend, despite the best efforts of the ACRL (Association of College and Research Libraries). For more on this subject and the ACRL's stance, see *College & Research Libraries News* 62, no. 3 (2001): 304–306.

But back to my mailbag. Respondents' opinions were starkly divided. Some applauded the piece for saying what they felt needed to be said. One disillusioned university librarian noted that too many colleagues were "blinded by prestige" and further opined that the "emphasis on scholarship seems to be hypocritical." Laura Wilkerson, *LJ's* Backtalk columnist (July 2001, 60), bluntly stated that "tenure for librarians stifles creative thought and dynamic growth and is anathema to the library spirit of democratic collectivity." Others—and here I happily run the risk of seeming self-serving—generously labeled it "brilliant." Those not sympathetic to either the substance or style of the piece used terms such as "diatribe," "nastiness," and "condescending dismissal" to convey their sense of anger, for anger, indeed, was the defining reaction in some quarters. And nowhere more so than in my own backyard.

Few of my status-conscious (but otherwise highly competent) librarian colleagues at Indiana University seem to agree with me on the irrelevance of faculty (or academic-related) status for librarians. Not only do they not share my views, but a few took such strong exception to the expression of opposing views that they vowed not to teach as adjunct faculty member in SLIS nor to contribute again to the school's fundraising campaigns. That, of course, is their right, but such reaction seems a tad strong.

However, pride of place in all of this huffing and puffing must go to the letter in support of faculty status sent by the Indiana University Bloomington chapter of the American Association of University Professors (AAUP) to *LJ*. As a card-carrying member of the AAUP, I found this especially rich. Now, you might be forgiven for thinking that the American Association of University Professors was an association of university professors. But you'd be wrong. Not satisfied with being overrepresented in faculty governance bodies, our status-starved colleagues have wormed their way into the ranks of the AAUP. The treasurer of my local chapter is, you've surely guessed, a librarian. The letter from the AAUP states that "Dean Cronin's AAUP colleagues at Indiana believe he misses the point on both tenure and governance issues."

What bothers me is the phrase "Dean Cronin's AAUP colleagues." Does that mean all my AAUP colleagues at Indiana University, a majority, or just some? Since, to the best of my knowledge, most of my faculty colleagues have probably never seen the article in question, it's a little naughty of my local chapter executive committee to presume to speak for the membership at large without so much as a "by your leave." Apparently, I fail to appreciate the fact that "academically trained librarians serve as faculty agents in voicing informed judgments on library development" and that academic status provides them with "protection against dismissal at the whim of administrators." Since many research libraries still don't grant faculty or academic-related status to their professional staff, we might expect to see evidence of whimsical dismissal in those institutions where our colleagues operate without metaphorical safety nets. But I've not seen the evidence, nor, I suspect, has anyone else. And then there is the comparative angle: why don't we find legions of summarily pink-slipped librarians dotting the landscape of the United

Kingdom, Germany, and other nations with comparable academic value systems and university library structures? Draw your own conclusions; I have long since drawn mine.

No doubt, boards of trustees and regents up and down the country can be persuaded, or hoodwinked, into granting some kind of watered-down academic status to librarians, but I doubt if most of them grasp fully the institutional implications of anointing librarians in this way. It's high time the issue was put back on the table.

REFERENCE

Cary, S. "Faculty Rank, Status, and Tenure." *College & Research Library News* 62, no. 5 (2001): 510–11, 520.

Since I wrote this coda, the AAUP has again invoked my name (see "Post-script to Plagiarism" later in this volume for the story) but this time siding with yours truly. So, hats off to my just-maligned AAUP colleagues for riding so spiritedly to my defense—and, it must be said, for the commendable consistency of their position on the matter of academic freedom.

THE VIEW FROM THE TRENCHES

Originally published June 2001

I've given scores if not hundreds of public presentations over the years. Among the most difficult was a recent one to a group of about three hundred paraprofessionals, the unsung toilers in the vineyards. How should I pitch my remarks so that I could navigate between the Scylla of the highfalutin and the Charybdis of condescension? It wasn't easy, and I don't know whether I succeeded, but it certainly was a salutary experience. It forced me to think back to my earliest days in the trenches and recall what the world looked like from the perspective of a tyro library assistant (as we were called in those days in the United Kingdom).

A couple of weeks ago while in London I visited Little Portland Street, two minutes from the bustle of Oxford Circus. My career began there, in a tiny branch library serving a rather curious user population, many of whom were drawn from the surrounding garment trade. The library is no more, having morphed into a restaurant. But my memories are fresh.

Much that we did was routine, numbingly so. Tasks were atomized and allocated strictly on the basis of rank and seniority within rank. One knew one's place in the pecking order, and there was a lot of pecking. A change in assignment brought me under the wings of a brace of professional librarians who encouraged me, as they did others, to experiment: handling complex reference queries, cataloging original materials, undertaking bibliographic detective work, and other Brahmanic tasks. The appetite was whetted, even if the spirit didn't exactly soar.

Almost thirty years later, the same frustrations and occasional sense of bitterness I experienced working with Westminster City Libraries greeted me in Cincinnati, as I chatted with the organizing committee of the one-day conference for paraprofessionals. Despite being a refreshingly spirited and committed group, it was clear that some, perhaps many, of them felt that they were underappreciated and inequitably rewarded for their services. Industry and demonstrable competence on the job were not enough: one had to have an accredited MLS under one's belt. Credentials, they believed, mattered more than performance. Yet, often it was they who gave the service its good name and kept the wheels running. Of course, this phenomenon is not peculiar to librarianship; social theorists have a lexicon to capture the frustrations of marginal groups in the workplace: the "sociology of the invisible," "invisible technicians," and "articulation work." But that's small consolation when you're stuck in the trenches.

John N. Berry III described something very similar in one of his editorials last year (*Library Journal*, October 1, 2000). Students at Dominican University's library science program told him just how unpleasant fieldwork experiences could be because of some professional librarians' status-consciousness and lack of hospitality. Why are some of our colleagues so ungracious and defensive? Are they merely trying to protect their financial investment in the MLS degree, or are they covering up for their own personal and/or professional inadequacies? Whatever the reason, it reflects badly on the wider community and perpetuates unhealthy stereotypes.

At Indiana University (IU), almost a third of our students graduate with an MIS (Master of Information Science) degree. Technically, it has been accredited by the American Library Association (ALA), but that is really neither here nor there. Most MIS students don't give a fig about ALA accreditation; some actually resent having their degree tainted by association. An MIS degree from IU certainly helps them get a foot in the career door, but it guarantees nothing. Success is contingent upon performance, and performance is a function of experience, capability, and motivation. These last three are not necessarily linked to possessing an ALA-accredited degree. Many of our MLS graduates, on the other hand, will only get a foot inside the chosen door by virtue of having an accredited degree, and once inside probably have a much more secure professional future ahead of them than some of their MIS peers who have to survive and thrive in more volatile marketplaces.

In an ideal world, we might (naïvely, I'll admit) expect those inside the polis to be rather more supportive and sympathetic of those locked outside the profession's walls by dint of not having a piece of parchment with the magic letters MLS inscribed on it. It has been some thirteen years since Elisabeth Davenport and I published *Post-Professionalism: Transforming the Information Heartland*, in which we made a case for removing the corsetry of accreditation and the other artificial barriers that control entry into the profession. Present practice is patently anachronistic and still pathetically protectionist, and I say that fully aware of the fact that programs such as my own are beneficiaries of the status quo.

Why not simply acknowledge competence and talent wherever it flowers and do what one can to cultivate the best possible mix of human intellectual capital within the wider ranks? That, at the risk of simplifying, is what a meritocracy is all about. Of all professions, should not librarianship be in the vanguard, welcoming proposals for change that would promote diversity (in the broadest sense of the term) and personal growth? Libraryland, surely, is no place for professional apartheid.

REFERENCE

Cronin, B., and E. Davenport. *Post-Professionalism: Transforming the Information Heartland*. London: Taylor Graham, 1988.

The Dreaded "L" Word

Originally published March 2001

You've seen the headline many times: "XYZ school drops 'L' word."
UW-Milwaukee was the latest, and it certainly won't be the last.
Each successive deletion brings forth a fresh fulmination from our
redoubtable editor-in-chief (John Berry III). And each defense of the
status quo is greeted with rapturous approval in the trenches. But
where did the "L" word expression come from, and, while we're on
the subject, who coined the term "Libraryland"? Granted, I once
claimed in the *Library Association Record* to have introduced Libraryland into the U.K. scene two decades ago, but that was only after en-
countering it in this country sometime in 1981. (Readers of the *Library Association Record* will be familiar with the whimsical jottings
of Edward Dudley in his regular column "Libraryland," while trivia
freaks will know that "Larkinland" refers to an entertainment based
on the poems of the popular English poet-librarian, Philip Larkin
[Thwaite 1992, 566, 581].) I first used "the 'L' word" in print in 1995,
but I don't know that I can claim originator status. In any event, the
term has grown legs, and pops up all over the professional literature. Indeed, it has become a powerful signifier of the ideological divisions within our ranks.

Many in Libraryland (a sane alternative to life in La La Land, it
must be said) take umbrage at the uppityness of their academic colleagues and their lexical snobbery. "What's wrong with the word 'library'?" they ask, puzzled and not a little embittered by the covert
campaign to erase the word from the titles of our schools. "Doesn't
it denote our areas of professional concern with remarkable clarity?"
"Don't people know exactly what a librarian is—which is more than
can be said for 'information scientist'?" "Isn't the library among the
most cherished of our national institutions—a symbol of enduring
democratic values?" And so on and so forth.

Lately, the "save the 'L' word movement" has found a rather effective ally. The fulminator-in-chief can now invoke the gravitas of Wayne Wiegand, UW-Madison's noted professor of library history. In a recent (October 27, 2000) op-ed in the *Chronicle of Higher Education*, Wiegand excoriated library and information science (LIS) programs for ignoring books and reading in their curricula. Since many LIS graduates still find (more or less) gainful employment in libraries, and since library patrons borrow and read books (it is still, by far, the dominant service function performed by public libraries), why are books and reading-related topics on the endangered species list? Why have arguably central concerns of the profession (what people read and why) been perversely marginalized by those of us ensconced in ivory towers?

Many moons ago, I worked in a large metropolitan library system. What struck me then was the familiarity my senior colleagues had with their stock (and I use the word "their" advisedly). They were of that generation for whom the appellation "bookman" was worn as a badge of honor. Of course, deep love for, and knowledge of, books didn't necessarily translate into outstanding service or patron-friendly environments. In general, public libraries (on both sides of the Atlantic) have become much more inviting and much less intimidating for the average user with the passing of our undoubtedly well-intentioned bookmen. The progressive democratization of the collection (lowest-common-denominatorizm, some might say) has, per force, reduced the need for staff with encyclopedic knowledge of books and their content. The "give the users what they want" approach to public service doesn't call for much in the way of bibliophily. Best-sellers and "Plumbing for Dummies" just fly off the shelves, which makes for a relatively easy professional existence.

Nonetheless, I have some sympathy for Wiegand's position, since understanding how users engage with texts (in the broadest sense of the term) is not only intrinsically interesting, but materially relevant to what we purportedly do in (parts of) our professional lives. Of course, a love for books is not something attending an LIS program will necessarily engender, though one hopes that it is, in some cases at least, a contributory reason for entering the profession. Many bookish souls are to be found working in bookstores of all stripes, eager to trade views and opinions with their customers. For all I know, the great majority of these will never darken the doors of a school, with or without the "L" word in its title, and they'll be none the worse for that. Their passion and knowledgeability, their love of the written word, will speak for themselves.

And it's here that I part company with the well-meaning Wiegand. The "value of stories," to appropriate his phrase, while a useful and attractive curricular component, is a manifestly inadequate base upon which to begin to construct a credible discipline, of the kind we these days variously label information science, information management, or information studies. Wiegand's interests can be most effectively embodied in a specialist degree (or boutique) program, such as that in book history and print culture at the University of Toronto, or similar programs offered by the Universities of London and Edinburgh. Lately, there has been a mini renaissance of interest in the sociocultural history of the book and the materiality of reading within academia. That is good news, indeed, but it won't be nearly enough to save the "L" word from being jettisoned by yet more LIS programs, as the field struggles to achieve some kind of structural stability and scholarly legitimacy in the upper echelons of the North American higher education system.

Libraryland, like Toyland, conjures up a host of warm and fuzzy images. But credible curricula need more than the kinds of fuzzy rhetoric and feel-good value statements so beloved of the American Library Association and other denizens of Libraryland. They require, inter alia, theoretical foundations and analytic rigor, ingredients that we don't usually associate with fantasy worlds—like Libraryland.

REFERENCES

Thwaite, A., ed. *Selected Letters of Philip Larkin 1940–1985*. London: Faber and Faber, 1992.

Wiegand, W. A. "Libraries Ignore the Value and Stories." *Chronicle of Higher Education* (October 27, 2000): B20.

POSTPROFESSIONALISM

It appears that I have a naïvely narrow view of what librarians do and the domain knowledge they bring to the exercise of their craft. According to an *LJ* Backtalk column ("Notes from a Not So 'Humble' Observer"), I'm suffering from "selective amnesia," since I seem to ignore services such as reference and genealogy in my recounting of the tasks performed by librarians. I can understand why Ms. Wilkerson, the author, feels as she does, but methinks she has read "The Dreaded 'L' Word" piece too literally.

In the interests of clarity, let's run the numbers. Unless I'm mistaken, activity-based costing and other performance measures tell us that book lending accounts for something like 80 percent of the services delivered by public libraries, and, unless I'm further mistaken, popular fiction and similar fodder account for the bulk of all materials borrowed by patrons. (If I'm hopelessly off the mark, feel free to write to *LJ* or just flame me.) Empirically, the principal function of public libraries is, still, to stock and lend popular stuff. Thus, much (not all, I readily concede) of what goes on in libraries is comparable with what happens in bookstores, or Wal-Mart, for that matter. This similarity increasingly invites questions like the following: If "Big Box Bookstores" can get by without hiring hoards of MLS-bearing assistants, why shouldn't that be the case in libraries? If retail bookstores can adjust their stock to reflect the demographics of the local community, why shouldn't libraries be able to do the same? The answer is simple. The Borders of this world don't employ MLS graduates to align stock with customer's needs and wants. Their managers are likely to have backgrounds in business administration, market research, and such like. So, one is tempted to ask, why don't libraries hire similar folk? The answer, of course, has little to do with the relative merits of potential candidates (or the relative attractiveness of the MBA vs. MLS); it has to do with protectionism. In Libraryland, the goal is not to hire the best person for the job, but the best person for the job *with* an MLS degree from an accredited program, who, as it happens, is more affordable than the typical MBA.

I don't for a minute mean to equate libraries with bookstores. In addition to their lending functions, public libraries, as Ms. Wilkerson reminds us, routinely perform a number of socially responsible services that no bookstore owner in his right mind would undertake. To the best of their ability they preserve aspects of the public record for the local community; they archive historical materials; they attempt to provide a general reference service for the community at large at no cost; and, unlike the average bookstore, will often strive to reflect the diversity of opinions on a topic, contentious or otherwise. Big Box Bookstores don't play in these arenas, because they are hopelessly labor intensive and revenue starved. So, if you're going to make a plea for investing in professionally qualified library personnel, it's likely to be in these more specialized areas, where domain-specific competencies come into play.

If I understand Ms. Wilkerson correctly, there is a felt need among paraprofessionals such as herself for more education and training in not only the techniques but also the history and philosophy of librarianship, and to that end schools such as mine should develop undergraduate programs. I both agree and disagree with her general point: to be sure, more could be done in terms of in-service training and library technician education to hone the skills of motivated paraprofessionals, but it is certainly not the role of graduate programs in research universities to undertake this function. A generation or two ago, undergraduate degrees in librarianship were commonplace. Today they have virtually disappeared from the face of the earth, only, and regrettably, to be supplanted in some cases by undergraduate programs in something called "information studies." Changing the label doesn't mask the fundamental limitations of such academically dubious offerings. Vocational degree programs of this kind have no place at the high tables of academia, belonging, as they do, to that class of education, which Cardinal John Henry Newman (1982) labeled "low Utilitarianism." Which is not to say that Ms. Wilkerson and her colleagues in the trenches don't deserve something better.

REFERENCES

Newman, J. H. *The Idea of a University.* Introduction and notes by M. J. Savage. Notre Dame, Ind.: University of Notre Dame Press, 1982.

Wilkerson, L. "Notes from a Not So 'Humble' Observer." *Library Journal* (July 2001): 60.

PROCESS FETISH

Originally published April 2001

Remember Churchill's telling aphorism, two nations divided by a common language? You say tomaaaayto and I say tomato, and all that jazz. I can live with your phonetic mutilation of tomatoes, forgive Quayle's orthographic abuse of the humble potatoe, and merely wince as the citizens of Plato's homeland are referred to as Greecians by the World's Most Powerful Man. However, such misdemeanors pale into insignificance alongside the treatment this enlightened nation bestows on that ostensibly innocuous word "process."

First, there's the matter of pronunciation . . . or egregious mispronunciation to be precise. A simple two-syllable term has been stretched on the tonsillar rack in mind-boggling fashion. The tortured end product sounds something like "prawwwwwwwwcess," and exhibits an elasticity unmatched by any other word in the American language—the rasping result of vowel lengthening combined with nasalization. A nameless professional colleague not only uses the word with greater frequency than any ("and," "for," and such like included) but distends it mercilessly, in ways I could not have imagined and the Inquisition would surely have applauded. Years of such caterwauling have taken their toll. I have developed a visceral aversion to the word "process" and all it represents—which brings me to the second point, namely, the fact that it stands for nothing at all, or, to be charitable, for everything.

If you think I'm exaggerating, or engaging in xenophobic twaddle, look and listen—to TV anchors, politicians, academics, not to mention your professional peers, in whose hands, so to speak, "process" has become the poster child of chicly sloppy speech. It's La-Z-Boy language at its worst, putting other established semantic substitutes like "thingy" and "stuff" firmly in the shade. It can, apparently, mean "event," "way," "mechanism," "device," "initiative," "approach," and countless other things, of which these are merely the least offensive examples. It's a Jack-of-all-trades noun cum verb; a pellet of puff prose that rises to the occasion before near instantaneous deflation. But, inevitably, wanton use leads to trivialization—Gresham's Law of public discourse, I suppose. I have sat through countless committee meetings, staying awake only by dint of process spotting. I once logged six in a single—admittedly serpentine and breathtakingly ungrammatical—sentence uttered by, well, I dare not say. . . . When I parsed this gem, it said exactly nothing. The empress was naked, but I'm not sure that anyone noticed. The intoning of "process," like a "hare krishna" mantra, had achieved the desired narcoleptic effect on the audience. In fact, the tactic was so effective that I can't recall what was actually said, just that it was process-rich.

Contemporary conversation is pebble-dashed with "process." It is an omnipresent default term, chameleonic in character, and probably very reassuring to a nation that, as any historian worth his or her salt will tell you, reveres what the term connotes. Process, and I speak as an avid, and sometimes open-minded, observer of the New World, seems to imply a vague admixture of collective participation, adherence to rules, and procedural transparency. Yet, it matters little if the outcome of any given process is daft or dubious, as long as the process whereby the process unfolded (if I may be permitted a moment's lampoonery) unfolded correctly. No "ends-justifying-the-means" nonsense here: what matters are the means to the end, even if there is no end. Indeed, the idea of outcomes is almost anathema to some of the most committed processualists I've come across over the years, not a few of whom are card-carrying ALA members. Since process is inherently good, then use of the word must be good, seems to be the underlying reasoning.

Predictably, for an erstwhile denizen of the Old World, I am occasionally perplexed by the cult of process worship on this side of the Atlantic. I have seen the American Library Association's (ALA) Committee on Accreditation rap a school over the knuckles for not dwelling enough on process. (Translation: have more faculty meetings even though the faculty doesn't feel a need for them; invent meaningless committee assignments so that more faculty can claim committee involvement.) Never mind that the school has a darn good program and an impressive track record; more important is the perceived failure to fetishize process. I sometimes think a school can have a mediocre program, but provided it shows evidence of dutiful commitment to process, it will receive a glowing report card.

Personally, I've stumbled at the altar of process on a couple of occasions. In my last decanal review, there was some tut-tutting because of my fondness for goal focusing rather than process focusing. I may be untutored in elementary civics, but I do occasionally glance at de Toqueville and I do appreciate the many strengths and attractions of, for instance, community-based government and university faculty governance, two notably process-conscious systems. Nevertheless, I'm still bamboozled by the fondness for folderol that characterizes so much routine debate in Libraryland (see Dean's List, *LJ*, March 15, 2001), where the mere invocation of the "P" word seems to confer instant legitimacy on a speaker and all that transpires. To slight the god of process (whether by omission or commission), is to risk excommunication from the fold.

These days, every Tom, Dick, and Harriet has to have his or her say, and there is clearly no such thing as too many cooks spoiling Libraryland's broth. Absolutely everyone has to be in on the act (read "process"). The result is glacial decision making combined with constipated policy formulation, served up in deathless prose. Just the stuff to warm the cockles of a Beltway insider's heart.

Since this piece was published, I have read somewhere that the British Prime Minister, Tony Blair, reportedly out-gaffed Vice President Quayle by thrice writing "toomorrow" in a note to a colleague. A slice of humble pie may be in order.

A Safe Haven

Originally published May 2001

Forgive me if this seems a tad provincial, but there is, ultimately, a serious point. I live in what amounts to a mid-sized university town, best known, it sometimes seems, for the oafish antics of its erstwhile basketball coach. These academic oases are quintessentially American. Bloomington, for instance, is an audacious blend of corn and cosmopolitanism. Grand opera (courtesy of the Indiana University Music School) and magnums of Château Latour live cheek by jowl with rednecks and fried catfish. Here, town and gown cannot pass like ships in the night: their fates are entwined. Yet, by golly, it all seems to work—most of the time, at any rate.

Slap bang in the middle of this particular oasis is our very own Taj Mahal, and I am not referring to one of the many exotic ethnic eateries which Bloomington boasts. This modestly sized wannabe airport terminal, architecturally just the right side of neobrutalism, is, in fact, the Monroe County Public Library. You can't miss it—which is probably just what the architect and staff were counting on. Its location is, arguably, its most important asset. Once inside, the interior design does its work. The building is spacious, luminous, well laid out, and accessible. It's like, well, an airport. And the people (those lurking behind desks and such like) seem eager to assist. As far as I can tell, there isn't a single "Silence please" sign blighting the landscape. Again, just like an airport. In short, the building doesn't conform to the popular stereotype or, to put it another way, it does: your interpretation will, naturally, reflect your particular parcel of prejudices.

Anyway, my children love it, and they're not without a modicum of discrimination. They can tell Harry Potter from Calvin and Hobbes at thirty paces. Nor are they blind to the blandishments of the local Borders or Barnes & Noble, from whom libraries could

50

learn a few lessons in the art of engineering ambience. For them, it's not a case of either/or. That shouldn't come as a surprise: for years researchers have told us that book buyers and book borrowers are by and large the same populations. And, more recently, it has been shown that Internet use and library patronage are significantly overlapping behaviors, albeit with considerably different emphases.

I've ambled around this space in tow and thrall. I actually thought of tape-recording the children's casual remarks and observations as they went about their business (it's the cultural anthropologist manqué in me, I suppose), but then thought the better of it. They know how to navigate the space; they seem manifestly at ease, and grateful for the plenitude on offer. They find stuff and stimulation. Going to the library constitutes a treat. It's not something they do because there are no bookstores, because we can't afford to buy books, or because their junior school doesn't have a library/media center. A trip to the library is something in its own right, an experience to be anticipated and enjoyed. It's the combination of space—safe space, most importantly—and stuff (stock, to use the posh term). And, additionally, the fact that they can take the stuff home by the ton and for free. It's a "no brainer," if I may slip into the demotic. Why wouldn't kids be attracted to libraries? And why wouldn't taxpayers see the wisdom of subsidizing the reading habit in the young? Why shouldn't these places be treated as protected social spaces?

I'll go so far as to say that one of the public library's key comparative advantages is the still credible perception that it affords one and all a safe and (in some cases, at least) inviting space. Right now, the London Borough of Lambeth is converting its old libraries into Idea Stores, in an imaginative partnership with commercial enterprises and educational institutions, in a determined effort to transform public perceptions and increase utilization rates. Libraries are a perfect example of "the third place," a necessary alternative to our workplace and domestic spaces. Paradoxically, the importance (perceived and actual) of physical space seems to be increasing in the electronic age. Libraries are scrambling to offer connectivity to those who may just find themselves on the wrong side of the putative "digital divide," in the process boosting the use made of both traditional (printed) and digital resources. Even academic librarians have grasped the importance of creating social spaces that support collaborative learning and informal interaction, involving not only students but also faculty (and library staff). As the library-without-walls mantra grows, the bricks and mortar continue to be laid down on our campuses with ever-increasing gusto.

Digitization clearly doesn't translate into demolition, and the irony is certainly not lost on academic administrators, who are frequently puzzled by the seeming illogicality (and expense) of it all. Tellingly, research library directors have been quick to appropriate the rhetoric of the digital commons, as a cunning rationale for helping push through new building and renovation projects. Watch as flash, but frequently threadbare, phraseology (think of "information literacy") is rolled out to legitimate growth agendas. I hope this doesn't backfire, because the issue of safe social spaces is too important to be sacrificed in the name of cant and careerism.

A COMMUNITY
INTELLIGENCE SERVICE

Originally published July 2001

There ain't nothing new under the sun. Well, of course there is, but just less than we imagined. The title of John Berry's April 1, 2001, *LJ* editorial—"The People's R&D Department"—caught my eye. It wasn't a paean to the research infrastructure of the People's Republic of China as I originally thought, but a revalorization of the role ascribed historically to public libraries in this country. I'll be the first to admit that "The People's R&D Department" is a clever moniker (so hats off to the elected selectman who came up with the coinage), but it's not entirely bereft of pedigree.

Some years ago I stumbled across a charming little book by one William Learned entitled *The American Public Library and the Diffusion of Knowledge*, which was commissioned by the Carnegie Foundation and published in 1924 by Harcourt. It struck me then as now as a remarkably farsighted and thoughtful volume. Now, you may recall that the March 1 issue of *LJ* had the subject of librarians and competitive intelligence (CI) as its cover story. CI is relatively new and exciting, as things go in Libraryland, except that it's not altogether new. More than seventy-five years ago, Learned was arguing the case for a "community intelligence service" staffed by a "trained intelligence personnel." Remember, this was long before the establishment of the CIA or FBI or most of the rest of the sprawling intelligence community, long before the Society of Competitive Intelligence Professionals (SCIP) came into being.

Noting the "daily losses in energy and material that result from sheer ignorance on the part of otherwise intelligent persons," he proposed the creation of a nationwide community intelligence service that would be "as familiar to every inhabitant as the local post-office and as inevitably patronized." This visionary service would be delivered by a new breed of information profession (Learned, of course, didn't use such a horrid neologism) whose value to the local community would be blindingly obvious. As he put it, "They would be like real pilots of its social, intellectual, and economic life—the linesmen alike of its material and spiritual power, bringing knowledge and need together." More to the point, these paragons of enlightened community service would not, in fact, be chips off the old block. "Mere grubbers in books according to professional tradition or a prevalent conception of a public librarian will not do," he goes on to say unabashedly. No doubt this recipe for success went down like the proverbial lead balloon in some quarters.

If 3M, Motorola, Microsoft, and most other Fortune 500 corporations are prepared to invest in competitive intelligence capability (and I'm not now talking about dumpster diving and the other ethically questionable CI activities that every so often garner media attention), why wouldn't the local community see the wisdom of exploiting to the fullest the array of information and knowledge resources at its disposal to improve the quality of life of its citizens? It's obvious. Or it ought to be.

All of which brings me to my colleague Rob Kling, the grand old man (in a manner of speaking) of social informatics. A few months ago, Rob gave a keynote address at the first Library Administration and Management Association (LAMA) Institute in Palm Springs. He chose to reflect on ways that librarians might position libraries relative to some of the shifts in information technology, and how they might deal with the emergence of new forms of competition, ranging from the Internet (doorstep delivery) to bookstores such as Borders (diversified, convivial ambience). One of his recommendations was that librarians should promote themselves to their patrons as "epistemic experts," highlighting their familiarity with the nature and sources of knowledge in myriad subject domains. That doesn't just mean assessing the relative value and reliability of one document/source over another, but teaching users how to select the best/most appropriate search engine for a certain type of search and explaining how websites are indexed and ranked.

He's convinced (though I'm less gung ho) that "librarians' epistemic expertise" is a meaningful and marketable concept that can be leveraged in such a way as to help the general public grasp the distinctive talents associated with a professionally qualified nongrubber of books. Whatever you may think, Kling's heart and instincts, like those of William Learned and the anonymous selectman of 2001, are in the right place. Maybe there is a value-adding role, in Kling's words, for "knowledge professionals who can help patrons find their way through both paper archives and technological mazes." And inevitably that role will need to be articulated compellingly as the in-house use made of library space and resources dwindles in the face of increasingly stiff competition from other infotainment providers and with the growth of distributed access to digital collections of all kinds.

Professional metaphors are ten-a-penny. These days the labels "information architect" and "information navigator" are vogue. Each rebranding of our spheres of professional activity has a life span of, typically, two to three years, before the next wave washes over the field. Yet, we could do much worse than recall the perspicacious Mr. Learned's pithy exhortation that librarians should be the linesmen connecting knowledge with need. Sometimes we need to look back in order to see the way ahead.

Peer Review and the Stuff of Scholarship

Originally published September 2001

Remember the old maxim, "Publish or perish"? Once upon a time, it was all very straightforward. People like myself were expected to publish stuff, either in respectable journals or with a reputable press. In academia, we all knew what it meant to publish, and we either stacked up or shipped out. Then along came the Web and, with it, new modes of prepublishing, posting, e-print archiving, "scholarly skywriting" (to use Stevan Harnad's charming coinage), and open peer review. Almost overnight, the rules of the game became less certain (just think of the Inglefinger Rule. See www.nejm.org/hfa /ingelfinger.asp). So, what does it mean to publish and who/what is a publisher in the digital age? What will change; what will persist?

Web-based publishing is a classic instance of technological substitution. Reduced entry costs and convivial technology have opened up the world of publishing to upstarts and new entrants of all stripes. In the digital age, anyone can be a do-it-yourself publisher; the vanity press has come into its own. Behind the sometimes excited rhetoric, the first real challenges to commercial publishers are being laid down. Most importantly, perhaps, technological change has triggered a perceptible shift in the moral economy of scholarly publishing. The seething anger felt by many academic librarians and a growing number of scholars at consistently greater-than-inflation journal price hikes by some commercial publishers has translated into action, most notably the formation of SPARC (Scholarly Publishing and Academic Resource Coalition), which elegantly defines its mission as striving to return science to scientists. SPARC, of course, is only one of many diverse electronic publishing initiatives that have sprouted up in recent years—think of PubMed Central—and some of these may (or may not) grow and institutionalize. In any event, their symbolic import is significant and they illustrate the radical changes occurring in the academic publishing ecosystem.

SPARC is deserving of serious attention because it demonstrates that value chain restructuring in the scholarly publishing business is more than a theoretical possibility. Some of us, of course, were vaguely aware of this long before the Web had really established itself. More than a decade ago, I wrote in the *British Journal of Academic Librarianship* ("Research Libraries: An Agenda for Change") that the solution to scholars' dependence on commercial publishers was "forward integration, with learned societies and/or universities becoming mainstream publishers. . . . An alternative would be the foundation of a number of university publishing consortia, or joint ventures." It may not have seemed obvious then, but it certainly does now. Let me be simple. People like me write stuff. The writing is subsidized by our universities. We give the stuff to commercial publishers (invariably waiving our copyright). Our universities buy back the stuff from the publishers so that we can read the stuff our colleagues write. Rocket science is not required to figure out that initiatives like SPARC or HighWire Press, which challenge the status quo, should be encouraged and their potential for scalability critically assessed.

Now, publishers aren't daft either, so they've been scrambling to exploit Web-based technologies to their advantage. A good example of "coopetition" is the open publishing initiative, CrossRef, which currently involves about seventy publishing houses. With the growth of multi- and interdisciplinary research, there is a need for maps, or path-finding tools, to promote "value mining" and foster discovery across databases/digital libraries. In short, scholars want to navigate the literature in ways that current tool sets and proprietary publishing practices don't readily permit. CrossRef, by offering citation linking across different publishers' wares, is a potentially important step in the right direction.

The Web is often hailed as a democratizing medium. The good news is that we can publish what we want; the bad news is that we can publish what we want. Opening the floodgates puts a premium on quality control. In academia, we call quality control peer review; when we're not producing stuff ourselves or consuming other people's stuff, we're vetting colleagues' stuff. Peer review is axial to scholarly publishing and the academic reward system—which, remember, determines who perishes. The peer review function will continue whether or not existing institutional arrangements are irrevocably broken or altered; publishers are not a necessary condition for the maintenance of peer review as traditionally conceived. Moreover, Theodore Bergstrom and others are probably right in thinking that commercial publishers may eventually have trouble exploiting the "free skilled labor" that referees, editorial board members and editors provide, given widespread concerns about price gouging and monopolistic practices.

It is quite possible that multilevel peer review will catch on in the context of Web-based publishing. However, it is unlikely that the academic reward system will decouple itself from peer review as we know it. But what about those high energy physicists who read and cite one another's e-preprints on arXiv.org, you say? How come they trust stuff before it gets into the journal of record? The brief riposte is that high energy physics (HEP) is a very tight, self-knowing community with intense internal vetting of research results. The stuff that emerges into the light of day has been rigorously scrutinized, even if it's not always in final form. Unfortunately, the cultural practices and social structures associated with the HEP community are not typical of scholarly communities in general, so we can't assume that what works for A will work for B, or C, or D. . . . For such reasons, I'd be very cautious about predicting the demise of peer review. Everything else may be flux in the publishing ecosystem, but peer review, in some recognizable form, will persist.

REFERENCE

Cronin, B. "Research Libraries: An Agenda for Change." *British Journal of Academic Librarianship* 4, no.1 (1989): 19–26.

THE END OF FIRST SALE

Originally published November 2001

Why is a book not like a car? Simple: Because you can't lease or rent a book—yet. We buy books from bookstores and we borrow books from friends and libraries, just as we purchase a new automobile or borrow a friend's car. But we don't usually talk of leasing or renting a book (circulating libraries being a thing of the past) in the sense that we might lease a Lexus from a dealership or rent a van from Hertz. When I buy a car, I can treat it (almost) the way I want; when I rent or lease one, certain restrictions come into play. I can't lend my Hertz van to friends, and it makes good sense to look after my Lexus so that I optimize the terms of the lease. However, when I buy a book, I can do what I want with it: I can annotate it, lend it, and, though I shouldn't, of course, copy it. Once I've handed over my money, the publisher is basically out of the picture. Publishers can't tell me how to treat the book or stop me circulating it to friends. Like the government, publishers are not welcome in our bedrooms. This ability (individual and institutional) to use and reuse books in unlimited fashion is enshrined in first sale doctrine.

In case you haven't guessed, I'm about to talk about e-books. Like many of you, I have been taking a more or less systematic interest in this topic for the past couple of years, struggling to see the wood as well as the trees. Two things have recently provided me with a sense of perspective and depth. The first was a conference on publishing in the twenty-first century, co-organized by the Library of Congress and the University of Virginia. I seemed to be the only speaker from academia on the program, the rest representing the vanguard of digital age publishing. It was something of an eye-opener to hear, for example, John Kilcullen, the ebullient CEO of Hungry Minds, on his company's innovative product development strategies, cobranding maneuvers, and obsessive customer focus. He peppered his remarks with the kind of comments that, coming from the mouths of others, might well have caused one to throw up: "The end game is to own the customer. . . . Mind share precedes market share." After listening to other pioneers, such as Tim O'Reilly of the eponymous Internet publishing company, I was left in little doubt that e-books and the world of recombinant, or customized, publishing would soon be here to stay. But not necessarily at the expense of printed books. E- and p-books will coexist for the foreseeable future.

After this seminar, the trees were much clearer but the wood was still fuzzy. Thanks to Clifford Lynch, the fuzziness has cleared and the wood is now sharply contoured. I've read numerous articles and opinion pieces on e-books, but none with the analytic rigor exhibited in Lynch's lengthy "Battle to Define the Future of the Book in the Digital World," which was recently published in *First Monday*. If you read only one professional article this month, let this be it.

The heart of Lynch's paper is not the description of the various e-book technologies, platforms, products, or standards, useful though those sections are. Rather, it is his explication of how e-books and the emerging apparatus of control—a closed consumer electronics system, aided and abetted by the U.S. Digital Millennium Copyright Act—may undermine the historic role performed by cultural heritage institutions such as libraries. Which brings us back to the principle of first sale, the "lifeblood of libraries . . . the framework that has historically allowed libraries to operate in America." What, Lynch asks, happens to libraries in a technologically controlled environment in which pay-per-view, transient access, and licensing options replace outright ownership and unlimited lending? Imagine an e-book future in which use, both personal and institutional, is tracked at the transaction level, where publishers monitor and model consumer behavior, and retain the ability to revoke access. This is fundamentally different from the world of p-books. Once I buy a book, there's no way the publisher is going to see it again; once a library buys a book, there's no way the publisher is going to restrict the number of loans. Not so in the world of e-books. Changes in the book production chain will trigger changes in the social value system.

Sticking with such a scenario, one can imagine publishers redirecting their wares away from traditional libraries to a new breed of middleman—a next generation netLibrary or ebrary. Just as the Hollywood movie studios use chains like Blockbuster to distribute their films to the domestic market, book publishers may choose to develop new distribution channels from which consumers buy, rent, download, or subscribe to/lease libraries of e-books. Imagine a Blockbuster, or equivalent, in which Stephen King's latest e-book sits side by side with the DVD of the movie version of his previous thriller, while public libraries are priced out of the secondary market for best sellers and new releases, and forced to make do with the publishers' e-crumbs.

Just as the music industry was terrified by the revenue-threatening prospects of Napster, the e-publishing business is haunted by the prospect of their goods, and presumptive profits, seeping uncontrollably into cyberspace. It is this fear that drives the quest for technologically propelled business models designed to protect and restrict peer-to-peer exchange of "soft goods," such as e-books. If publishers are able to seal and secure their intellectual assets against unsanctioned copying and distribution, then, ultimately, it may mean the end of the first sale doctrine in the world of bookselling. This prospect has potentially profound implications for libraries.

REFERENCE

Lynch, C. "Battle to Define the Future of the Book in the Digital World." *First Monday* at www.firstmonday.org/issues6_6/lynch/index.html (accessed August 15, 2002).

THE DIGITAL DIVIDE

Originally published February 2002

Don't underestimate the importance of alliteration to public policy. The euphonious "digital divide" has caught the fancy of policy wonks as much as the information community. In fact, you'll encounter the term just as often inside the Beltway as along the lanes of Libraryland. It is a powerful metaphor that has successfully captured the public's attention. It's also a great way of securing federal funding or local sponsorship for a well-intentioned e-project or online community intervention. This is as true in the United Kingdom as the United States.

The digital divide phenomenon is not exactly new. In the late eighties and early nineties, it was fashionable to talk of the information rich and the information poor, but then along came the public Internet and World Wide Web. These developments helped make visible the information gap between the "haves" and the "have-nots." Measurable differences in ownership of computers, access to information technology, and baseline indicators of Internet connectedness have powerfully illuminated the gulf between elite and marginal groups, both within and across societies. They bring the rhetoric of info rich/info poor incontestably to life, helping to get the issue of distributive injustice on the radar screens of the people who purportedly matter. The digital divide has quickly become a universal shorthand for variations in Internet-related access and usage patterns that are, residually, attributable to socioeconomic factors.

Of course, the digital divide is a manipulative misnomer, runs the familiar conservative refrain. It conveniently overlooks the fact that wealth, especially in the United States, is distributed in massively unequal fashion. If BMWs, Rolexes, and Floridian penthouses are unequally distributed, why on earth would we expect ownership of ICTs (information and communications technologies) to be less asymmetrical? So, if we're going to bleat on about divisions within society, why not begin by acknowledging that stratification is structural, and that there's no especially good reason to privilege things digital? This kind of bluster may work on the hustings, but it is socially myopic. Providing subsidies for Internet access through, say, public libraries, is not quite the same thing as doling out BMWs to those on the welfare rolls. ICTs are key elements of our emerging sociotechnical infrastructure; not to have access, whether by choice, lack of means, or because of unenlightened public policy, means that individuals miss out on opportunities for personal and collective growth. Eliminate the divide, and everyone benefits, runs the counterrefrain. Fortunately, it's easier (and considerably cheaper) to bring citizens online than distribute BMWs to the masses. Whereas the relative cost of a Bimmer doesn't vary greatly year on year, the costs of consumer communication technologies (radio, TV, phone, etc.) have a marked tendency to decline steeply over time until, in this country at least, blanket household penetration has been achieved.

Federal government has caught the digital divide bug in a big way. The U.S. Department of Commerce's National Telecommunications and Information Administration (NTIA) has published a series of reports on the digital gap, graphically entitled *Falling through the Net*. The fourth in this series, which has the subheading *Toward Digital Inclusion*, shows, contrary to widespread belief, that the divide between the "haves" and "have-nots" is closing rapidly. In August 2000, 58 percent of U.S. households had Internet access. In the same month, 116.5 million Americans were online at some location. The report notes that certain sections of society that have traditionally been beyond the digital pale (e.g., low-income groups, ethnic minorities, women) are making dramatic gains, though some others, notably Blacks and Hispanics, remain underrepresented even after income and educational differences are factored into the analysis. The findings of the NTIA report provide cause for cautious optimism, and a strong reminder of the role to be played by libraries and other public agencies in facilitating participation among those without the means or technical ability to go online independently. At the same time, the report should encourage us to exercise caution in uncritically evoking the notion of a digital divide. It should also cause us to define our terms in such a way that the multiple bases of marginalization are better acknowledged. For instance, among the excluded may be those who have some kind of disability, and for whom assistive technologies and appropriate Web page design policies can make a world of difference.

The picture that emerges from the NTIA is not replicated in most other countries. Even in some relatively advanced nations, the gaps are still quite striking. In Britain, it is estimated that more than 60 percent of the richest 10 percent of the population has household access to the Internet, while only about 6 percent of the poorest 10 percent has online access. Once we move to the Third World, the digital disparities are mind-boggling; most people don't even have a phone, let alone an online connection, either at work or home. As Alberto Manguel (2001) put it recently, "For millions of human beings on this planet, the Web is as inaccessible as the universe's farthest moon." According to a recent study by Mike Jensen, "The African Internet: A Status Report," there are about 4 million Internet users in the continent, of whom 2.5 million are in South Africa. In Africa, one in every 200 persons has Internet access compared with 1 in 30 globally, and 1 in 3 in advanced economies. It is in this context that I think the concept of a digital divide still has considerable mileage, and one can but hope that the policy experts won't lose interest in the subject once domestic inequalities begin to be eradicated. After all, it makes little sense for a world power to be communicating largely with itself. So, with that in mind, let me reintroduce you to Metcalfe's law, which states that the power of a network increases in proportion to the square number of nodes on the network. Policy wonks take note!

REFERENCES

Jensen, M. "The African Internet: A Status Report," at www3.wn.apc.org/africa/afstat.htm (accessed August 15, 2002).

Manguel, A. "The Library of Robinson Crusoe." *The American Scholar* (winter 2001): 61–70.

CELEBRITY CHALLENGED

Celebrity is the undisputed coin of the realm. These days, pedigree, education, aesthetic sensibility, and moral authority count for very little. In the United States, nothing matters more than celebrity, except perhaps really, really serious wealth. Now, old money knows its place, and studiously shuns the limelight (Aldrich 1996). It's new money that seeks out celebrity and it's would-be celebrities who pursue photo-op riches. And it's not just the United States. The malaise is spreading. The emergence of a celebitocracy can be seen in the United Kingdom, Australia, and Spain, to name but three countries. It's not a pretty sight. The globalization of *Hola!* magazine and its polyglot derivatives provides a platform for parvenus and minor royals to garner a few pieces of silver for gleefully exposing their lack of taste to the masses. A veritable media industry has developed to support the insatiable craving for instant celebrity—both demand and supply side. Today's generation, most of whom wouldn't know a Warhol from a warthog, pathetically wants their fifteen minutes of fame.

Once upon a time, celebrities were, well, celebrities. They were public officials, sportsmen, divas, or military leaders who stood apart, and they were in relatively short supply. Celebrity status was usually earned, not engineered or bought. Today, the vast majority of so-called celebrities are merely famous for being famous: for posturing, posing, or pontificating. This is an age in which news about news anchors is deemed more newsworthy than news. Vacuity has been parleyed into a minor art form, with not a little help from agents, PR gurus, and shameless spin doctors. The scramble for the limelight has intensified mightily, such that celebrities see themselves as a caste apart from mere "civilians," the term coined, I believe, by the pouting Elizabeth Hurley for those of us beyond the celebrity pale. In an "economy of attention," to use the late Herb Simon's apt term, the trick is to wrest the spotlight away from other wannabe celebs and corral as may eyeballs as possible. This may mean demeaning the Dalai Lama, flamboyantly (re)entering rehab, or simply dropping one's pants. The inflationary spiral is inexorable, and tomorrow's celeb will have to exhibit considerable verve to stay one step ahead of the pack, as Martin Amis (2001, xii) noted recently: "You can become rich without having any talent (via the scratchcard and the rollover jackpot). You can become famous without having any talent (by abasing yourself on some TV nerdathon: a clear improvement on the older method of simply killing a celebrity and inheriting the aura)."

Even academia is not immune to the siren call of celebrity and there is much interest in the emergence of academic stars, superstars, and megastars (Spurgin 2001), a cross between celebrity and public intellectual (think of Stanley Fish or Cornel West). Recently, one of Columbia University's stellar professors, Edward Said, was involved in a high-profile rock-throwing escapade on the Lebanon-Israel border. Intriguingly, the pro-Palestinian professor's concrete expression of animus towards Israeli soldiers was defended by his employers. To the bewilderment of some, Columbia University decided to take no action against the celebrity professor. The notion of academic freedom clearly has considerable elasticity in some parts of New York City. (For a flavor of the debate, take a look at the "Letters" pages of *Academic Questions* 14, no. 2, [2001]: 5–12.)

How is Libraryland responding, given this widespread trend? Are we producing our quota of public intellectuals, *philosophes*, technology pundits, and media headliners? The answer is a resounding no. The celebritization of Libraryland is a long way off (Cronin and Shaw, 2002). That is both good news and bad. It's good in that we don't (yet) have paparazzi doggedly pursuing ALA presidential candidates and we don't have the center pages of *LJ* and *American Libraries* given over to showcasing the homes of prominent metropolitan library directors. Libraryland is still resolutely dull and devoid of sparkle: flashbulbs pop ever so demurely at our major gatherings, and a picture in *AL* of an ALA staffer waltzing with a professional colleague is as close as we get to the kind of coverage beloved of *People* magazine. We don't have a local celebrity culture (Laura Bush is about as close as one comes). Nor do we have an enfant terrible worthy of the name on the professional horizon.

The sad thing is that we have no celebrities of substance either, unless one counts the nominal Librarians of Congress, scholars such as Daniel Boorstein or James Billington. But, strictly speaking, these are insider-outsiders. Libraryland really doesn't have a single public intellectual—a dying breed, according to Furedi (2001)—worthy of the name in its ranks: no one like Daniel Patrick Moynahan, Susan Sontag, or Noam Chomsky, not even a homegrown version of social wave theorist Alvin Toffler. There are no spokespersons in Libraryland who contribute influentially to national debates on the issues of the day, whose pronouncements, oracular or otherwise, help shape public opinion. Given that the profession likes to see itself as a bastion of democratic values and social inclusion, this silence is all the more perplexing. Nor, for better or worse, does Libraryland have its equivalents of Johnnie Cochrane or Dr. Jack Kevorkian, individuals who raise social issues while at the same time adroitly, if luridly, raising their personal and professional salience. Sound bites about libraries, books, reading, and related matters are more likely to be uttered by outsiders than eminent (or not so eminent) librarians. The only individual whose views seem to attract fitful local and national media attention is Nicholson Baker, another outsider.

Our absence from the public stage is dispiriting, and small consolation for avoiding the excesses of the celebrity culture. Perhaps we should dust off and dip back into our copies of *High Visibility: The Making and Marketing of Professionals into Celebrities*, coauthored by the doyen of the field, Philip Kotler (1997). Or, and somewhat more challenging, perhaps we might think about how we could recruit more visible and high-minded individuals into the profession.

REFERENCES

Aldrich, N. W. *Old Money: The Mythology of Wealth in America*. New York: Allworth, 1996.

Amis, M. *The War against Cliché: Essays and Reviews 1971–2000*. New York: Hyperion, 2001.

Cronin, B., and D. Shaw. "Banking (on) Different Forms of Symbolic Capital." *Journal of the American Society for Information Science and Technology* 53, no. 13 (2002).

Furedi, F. "An Intellectual Vacuum." *The Times Higher Education Supplement* (October 5, 2001): 17. See also Grafton, A. "The Public Intellectual and the American University." *The American Scholar* 70, no. 4 (2001): 41–54; and for a fuller treatment of the subject, Posner, R. A. *Public Intellectuals: A Study of Decline.* Cambridge, Mass.: Harvard University Press, 2001.

Kotler, P., I. J. Rein, and M. Stoller. *High Visibility: The Making and Marketing of Professionals into Celebrities.* New York: McGraw-Hill, 1997.

Spurgin, T. "The *Times* Magazine and the Academic Megastars." *The Minnesota Review* 52–54 (2001): 225–38.

POSTMODERN PERIPHRASIS

For no good reason I've taken to reading the *PMLA* (*Publications of the Modern Language Association of America*), and it's proving to be an eye-opener. Here, postmodern pretentiousness and political correctness fuse sublimely. In the pages of the *PMLA*, po-mo scholars po-facedly roll out their frequently threadbare lexicon: find me an article without words like "privileging," "hegemony," "otherness," "problematized," "ethnicized," "intertextuality," "dialogism," and "simulacra," or an author who doesn't genuflect at the altar of French pseudophilosophy, and I'll buy you the complete works of Lacan—in translation, of course. It's the literary equivalent of drawing by numbers. I admit that it's easy to sneer, and sneering will be dismissed airily as a patriarchal response by the ruling elites within departments of English, cultural studies, and kindred disciplines. But sneer one must, despite the occasionally lustrous writing to be found in the pages of the *PMLA*.

This, however, is just the tip of the iceberg. Who can forget the wonderful hoax in which the physicist, Alan Sokal (1996), published his nonsensical article, "Transgressing the Boundaries: Toward a Transformative Hermeneutics of Quantum Gravity," in the cultural studies journal *Social Text* with the effusive blessing of the unsuspecting referees? The laudable Sokal subsequently combined forces with his French physicist colleague, Jean Bricmont, to produce "Fashionable Nonsense: Postmodern Intellectuals' Abuse of Science" (Picador 1999), a rigorous debunking of bankrupt critical studies scholarship in Europe and North America. Given the scale and egregiousness of the problem they exposed, Sokal and Bricmont showed remarkable restraint, resisting the temptation to scoff. Which brings us back to the *PMLA*, and a wondrously entitled article by Arturo

Arais (2001), "Authoring Ethnicized Subjects: Rigoberta Menchú and the Performative Production of the Subaltern Self."

You may be familiar with the *scandale* surrounding the "factuality" of RM's acclaimed testimonial, "I, Rigoberta Menchú," even if you haven't read her autobiographical account of the struggle in Guatemala. Apparently, her tale doesn't quite fit the facts, or the facts don't quite fit her tale. An intense scholarly debate consequently erupted over the issues of trust, authenticity, and the "truth effects" of testimonials. To quote Arias (76), "[t]he debate has centered on whether Menchú told the truth in her book." For most of us, it's a pretty straightforward matter to acknowledge that something is either true or false especially when confronted with the evidence. Not so for some postmodern scholars. Menchú, we are told, is using "discourse strategically" (76), and our uncomfortableness with this fact arises from "unresolved contradictions in the cultural logic of the West" (83).

I'm all for nuanced analysis and culturally sensitive interpretations of human behaviors and historical events, but I don't believe that interpretative tolerance requires that we debase language and subvert common sense. Menchú's account is either inherently true or not. Of course, one acknowledges that autobiographies will often exhibit some degree of amnesia and selective highlighting, but that need not undermine their essential trustworthiness. If, however, her account lacks credibility, we can presumably adduce reasons and justifications (Arias invokes "the polysemy of language" and "the slippages inherent in translation," 76), but without resorting to the semantic contortions which have the author and some of his colleagues fabricating weasel words like "strategic discourse" to dig themselves out of a tight spot. Arias concludes his defense of Menchú by stating (87) that "the indigenous subject [RM] is held up to a standard of truth that those who flaunt other discourses have never had to meet." One wonders what precisely is mean by "flaunt other discourses" and just whom he has in mind. But the pièce de résistance is surely the concluding sentence (87) of this tortuous defense of relativism: "If her text, which did not make any historical truth claims, achieved the goals of ending massacre and creating respect for Mayan culture, does it matter if it did not conform to how Western science contextualizes documentary facts?"

This impassioned legitimizing of "means justifying the ends" contains an out-of-the-blue allusion to Western science which, as far as one can tell, is being castigated for its inhospitableness toward "zigzagging narrative logic" written from "a crypto-feminist subaltern perspective" (81). But Western science, *pace* Mr. Arias, has nothing to do with Menchú's storytelling or its truth-quotient. One is struck reading this and so much other postmodernist scholarship by the unwitting (and here I'm being charitable) appropriation of indigenous, zigzagging narrative logic by those who should know better. Arturo Arias does Menchú a disservice by resorting to periphrasis. Why not call a spade a spade, or at least a shovel? Strategic discourse is an arch circumlocution for being economical with the truth. When Goebbels did it for the Third Reich, we called it propaganda; when Dick Morris did it for former President Clinton, we called it spin doctoring; when Clinton did it for himself, we called it lying. Why privilege [*sic*] Menchú?

The sorry state of literary (and cultural) studies in North America can be gleaned from the pages of the *PMLA*: group adherence to a pretentious and inelegant lexicon, paradigmatic myopia, and, occasionally, plain silliness. In Martin Amis's (2001, xiii) understatement, "[a]cademic preferment will not come from a respectful study of Wordsworth's poetics; it will come from a challenging study of his politics—his attitude to the poor, say, or his unconscious 'valorization' of Napoleon." For an elegiac account of the decline and fall of departments of literature in American universities and the insidious effects of unbridled epistemic relativism, I heartily recommend Alvin Kernan's (1999) *In Plato's Cave*. Kernan most certainly does not write by the numbers.

No wonder Sokal and others (e.g., the National Association of Scholars, www.nas.org/) have broken the silence: the emperors have no clothes. However, if "objective realism" (of the Sokalian variety) is not to your taste, and you have some reservations about extreme "epistemic relativism," then there's always "socially responsible realism," as advocated recently by Maureen Linker (2001). I can't say fairer than that, can I?

REFERENCES

Amis, M. *The War against Cliché: Essays and Reviews 1971–2000.* New York: Hyperion, 2001.

Arias, A. "Authoring Ethnicized Subjects: Rigoberta Menchú and the Performative Production of Subaltern Self." *PMLA* 116, no. 1 (2001): 75–88.

Kernan, A. *In Plato's Cave.* New Haven, Conn.: Yale University Press, 1999.

Linker, M. "Epistemic Relativism and Socially Responsible Realism: Why Sokal Is Not an Ally in the Science Wars." *Social Epistemology* 15, no.1 (2001): 59–70.

Sokal, A. "Transgressing the Boundaries: Toward a Transformative Hermeneutics of Quantum Gravity." *Social Text* 46/47 (1996): 217–52.

Sokal, A., and J. Bricmont. *Fashionable Nonsense: Postmodern Intellectuals' Abuse of Science.* New York: Picador, 1999.

PLAGIARISM AND
POLITICAL CORRECTNESS

As I write, William Jefferson Clinton (WJC) is demitting presidential office. His approval ratings are high; his reputation tarnished. This is happening in the same week that we celebrate Martin Luther King Jr. (MLK) day. Speaking as a resident alien, it is hard not to be struck by the variable standards applied to these two individuals (albeit individuals from different eras) and wonder what this tells us about the construction of public reputation in contemporary American society. The hagiography of MLK continues, while the vilification of WJC shows little sign of abating. In saying this, I am making no moral, or comparative, judgment whatsoever. It is, however, most revealing, and I want to use King's case, specifically his well-documented record of plagiarism, to illustrate the corrosive effects of politically correct (PC) thinking within academia.

A decade or so ago, *The Journal of American History* (*JAH* 78, no. 1 [1991]) published a number of papers on King's plagiarism. Large chunks of MLK's Ph.D. thesis at Boston University were copied without appropriate attribution, a practice that continued with his speeches and sermons, including the "I Have a Dream" speech. The editor of *JAH* took considerable effort to set King's misdemeanors in their historical and cultural contexts. Of course, King's plagiarism, which was eventually, if reluctantly, acknowledged by his professors, Boston University, and the MLK Papers Project at Stanford University, doesn't diminish one iota his historical stature. However, the last thing MLK needs is misguided, revisionist history; his death in the cause of social justice transcends everything else.

Martin Luther King Jr., a man of the cloth, was not without human frailties, as David Levering Lewis, the MLK Jr. Professor of History at Rutgers University, illustrated in his contribution to the *JAH* special issue. Are we to overlook King's "reputed tomcatting" (*JAH*, 82), while castigating the errant Clinton? Little is heard these days of MLK's alleged philandering, while WJC's reputation is indelibly stained by his high-profile womanizing. (Clinton, of course, is not the only public figure in the United States to have a strong libido, as Joe Eszterhas so rivetingly and scabrously revealed in *American Rhapsody*.) Here, I am commentating on the commentators, for not a few of whom ahistoricism seems to be the favored disposition. *Autres temps, autres moeurs* is the highbrow way of saying that things were different then. To me, at least, it seems inconsistent, whether the issue is plagiarism, infidelity, or any other human failing.

Why should Dr. Martin Luther King Jr.—and one cannot but notice the now ritualized prefixing of MLK's name with "Dr."—warrant a different standard of treatment? It is particularly unfortunate that the near-universal insistence on referring to MLK as "Dr." should persist even after the truth about his plagiarism has been established. Yet, the palpable irony of this situation seems to go unnoticed by some. If others in the academy, be they students or faculty, are held to the highest standards in the matter of credit giving, why should MLK be held to a lower standard? In academia, the sin of plagiarism is inexcusable, the sanctions severe. It is revealing that MLK's transgressions were at first airbrushed out of the history books, then "explained" as a culturally acceptable form of "intertextualization," "voice-merging," or "synthesizing," to mention but three of the circumlocutions adopted by his defenders and chronicled by Theodore Pappas in his book, *Plagiarism and the Culture War*. (I am reminded here of a comment made by Neil Postman [1999, 78]: "You can 'deconstruct' *Mein Kampf* until doomsday and it will not occur to you that it is a paean of praise to the Jewish people. Unless, of course, you want to claim that the text can be read as irony, that Hitler is spoofing anti-Semitism.")

King's transgressions matter far less than the reaction to the revelation of his crimes/mistakes. The blatant double standard tells us a lot about how society works. Scholars' careers have been seriously damaged as a result of proven plagiarism. The mere imputation of plagiarism can be the kiss of death for a faculty member or doctoral student, and most certainly not a charge to be uttered lightly— which is precisely why it is a favored means of attacking one's foes. What MLK engaged in was not unconscious remembering of another's ideas or words, nor (just) permissible paraphrasing: it was plagiarism, a word many of his possibly well-intentioned but seriously misguided defenders seemed incapable of uttering once the story broke, as Pappas unflinchingly described.

Why, then, do we demonize WJC, but see, hear, and speak no evil when it comes to MLK? Even the *Encarta* encyclopedia entry dealing with his education sidesteps the issue of intellectual theft. MLK remains unscathed on both the personal and professional fronts. Why is King granted Teflon-coated, iconic status and Clinton treated as fodder for the *National Enquirer*? It is hard to accept that the difference in reception granted these two larger-than-life figures is simply a matter of a generational shift in journalistic conventions. Something deeper—political correctness—is at work, and its not so pale reflection can be seen in our own field. More specifically, it seems that issues of race in the United States are occasionally so sensitive as to be well nigh unmentionable. This point is made in Katharine Jones's (2001, 169) recent sociological analysis of English identity in the United States.

> The English people I spoke to developed the idea that America was more "raced" than England by pointing out how seriously race is taken in the U.S. They argued that the discourse about race did not allow for any questioning of the status quo. Imogen noted that people "jump[ed] down my throat" when she asked what she thought were innocent questions about race relations in the U.S., such as "why black people have to be called African Americans." She noted, "there is a tension, and . . . you can't speak your mind about it. You can't even let yourself think about the issues; you can't even investigate the issues here, for fear of offending somebody."

Several years ago (Cronin, 1995, 46), I commented on the polluting effect of politically correct language within the library and information science (LIS) field. I described it as "absolutist, hectoring, self-deluding, and frequently illogical in character." Such discourse is part of the same sorry phenomenon I have just sketched in relation to MLK, a phenomenon exquisitely dissected by Kors and Silverglate (1998). If you really want to get a feel for the "politicized perversion of language" (193) so prevalent on our campuses today, you can do no better than read this searing indictment of PC wackiness. For instance, on the subject of diversity they note (193) that universities "operate with a humanly impoverished notion of 'diversity,' excluding personality, social class, spirituality, taste, and private passions." Their wide-ranging analysis certainly helps one understand the driving motivations of those who would like to pasteurize the legend of MLK. It should also act as a wake-up call for those in our field who do not want to see academic standards and professional norms terminally debased by political correctness and "Orwellian overreaching" (Kennedy 2002, 146).

REFERENCES

Cronin, B. "Shibboleth and Substance in North American Library and Information Science Education." *Libri* 45, no.1 (1995): 45–63.

Eszterhas, J. *American Rhapsody.* New York: Vintage Books, 2001.

Jones, K. *Accent on Privilege: English Identities and Anglophilia in the U.S.* Philadelphia, Pa.: Temple University Press, 2001.

Kennedy, R. *Nigger: The Strange Case of a Troublesome Word.* New York: Pantheon, 2000.

Kors, A. C., and H. A. Silvergate. *The Shadow University: The Betrayal of Liberty on America's Campuses.* New York: Free Press, 1998.

Pappas, T. *Plagiarism and the Culture War.* Tampa, Fla: Hallberg, 1998.

Postman, N. *Building a Bridge to the 18th Century: How the Past Can Improve Our Future.* New York: Vintage Books, 1999.

Postscript to Plagiarism

Library Journal declined to publish "Plagiarism and Political Correctness." Rightly or wrongly, I felt the piece was turned down because of its potentially controversial content. *LJ* can, of course, speak for itself, and might, for instance, respond that the subject matter was inappropriate for my column, or that the topic had already been covered adequately in the library literature and elsewhere. In any event, I approached my local colleagues in the Association of American University Professors asking them to write to *LJ* expressing our collective concern at what appeared to be an instance of censorship by a professional journal, ironically one that prided itself on being unwaveringly committed to freedom of information and freedom of expression. To their credit, the Bloomington Executive Committee of the AAUP wrote a doughty letter, which noted that the magazine appeared to have "fallen short in promoting and protecting academic freedom." Presumably, I could have resigned on the spot as a matter of principle and, presumably, the editors of *Library Journal* could just as easily have chosen not to renew my contract. I didn't, and they didn't. Clearly, we deserve one another.

Amazons R Us

Originally published October 2001

Note that I have corrected the misattributions and misspellings made in the published version of this, about which more in the follow-on piece.

"What would a feminist IT look like?" Not my question, but a discussion topic on Hope Olson's course syllabus, Feminism and Library and Information Studies, taught at the University of Alberta's School of Library and Information Science. Variations on this question are in vogue. If you'd really like to know the answer to Professor Olson's question, let me suggest that you come to IU and take Gender and Computerization (G&C). The course is taught by my colleague Susan Herring, a linguist and widely recognized authority on gender and computer-mediated communication. G&C is a rigorous course, theoretically framed and empirically informed. It addresses serious social issues in a scholarly fashion. Let me quote from the outline: "This course explores the relationship between information and communication technology (ICT) and the gender of people who design, use, administer, and make policy concerning computer systems and computer networks such as the Internet." Naturally, I welcome research and teaching that systematically address structural gender bias in our daily lives, but I make a clear distinction between scholarship and the kind of speculation masking as scholarship that pollutes Libraryland these days.

Feminism has its good side and its bad side. The systematic investigations of scholars like Professor Herring represent the good. Now for the not so good: A decade or so ago, Roma Harris wrote a book entitled *Librarianship: The Erosion of a Woman's Profession* (there's nothing like nailing your flag firmly to the mast) in which she vaunts "the female traditions of library work" and the "female identity of the profession." But she doesn't stop there. Her rallying cry to the ALA

(American Library Association) and kindred bodies is "to become feminist associations," no less. The redoubtable Camille Paglia has referred to this kind of misguided and regressive thinking as "infirmary feminism," a term I rather like. However, Professor Harris doesn't take the proverbial biscuit, despite her unabashed commitment to agency and activism. That honor goes to Karen Schneider for an exhortation and to Sarah Pritchard for a question (1994, 42–45). The exhortation runs thus: "If we believe in ourselves, our profession, and the people we serve, we have a moral responsibility to become Amazons with laptops." Well, I, for one, feel no categorical imperative to become an Amazon waving my laptop in the air, and I sincerely hope that applies for the majority of *LJ's* readership. Next, the question which helped Ms. Pritchard share the biscuit: "[H]ow can the profession be sexist, when it is female-dominated?" Right on! For anyone interested in finding out more, a selection of Ms. Pritchard's writings can be found on the Web page of the ALA's Committee on the Status of Women in Librarianship.

But back to Professor Olson, whose syllabus provides cynics like myself with opportunities for enlightenment. Apparently, what I and other middle-aged, White, male, canon-hugging Neanderthals lack is a feminist poststructural epistemology. In a nutshell: knowledge is discursively constructed and truth is pluralistic. Or, to put it another way, anything goes . . . and all voices are equal. That, it seems, is the message being sent by Ms. Olson to her students. But, of course, all views and voices are not equal nor, perish the thought, should they be. And librarians, arguably more than almost any other professional tribe, should be aware of the need for rigor, discrimination, and selectivity in the exercise of their craft. Unfortunately, some of the feminist rhetoric swirling around Libraryland is an open invitation to rampant relativism. One sees it in the area of collection development and management and the pernicious assaults on the Western literary and musical canon. And I see it in my neck of the woods.

I routinely act as a referee or reviewer for scholarly and professional journals. In recent years, I have been struck by the rising tide of uncritical, cookie-cutter articles invoking "isms" emanating from our library schools. Feminism (or, "feminisms," as Hope Olson would have it) is, of course, right up there at the top of the list, closely followed by, and sometimes accompanying, constructivism. It seems to me that we are witnessing the social construction of absolutely everything, gender included. But then, as Ian Hacking asks in his wonderfully even-handed book, *The Social Construction of What?* "If gender is, by definition, something essentially social, and if its is constructed, how could its construction be other than social?" (39). Judging by some of the faculty and doctoral student work which flows across my desktop, basic questions such as this go unasked and unanswered. That's depressing.

Argumentation is replaced by assertion; evidence by ideology. Try this specimen for size. Writing in *Progressive Librarian*, Roma Harris informs us that "old-style librarians" are being replaced by "new male-style [*sic*] information specialists," who apparently "promote a vision of the virtual library in which direct human contact is replaced with access to fast computerized information networks, financed on a per-use basis." One might be forgiven for asking what a "male-style information specialist" actually is, and what evidence she has to support her subsequent claim that this interspecies has been somehow seduced by information technology. The self-serving picture she paints is painfully at odds with the collage of professional images and impressions I take away from the pages of *LJ*, *American Libraries,* and the rest of the professional literature I consume. It is also sharply at odds with the feedback I derive from professional colleagues who work in the real world. But perhaps we are just going to have to accept that feminist poststructural epistemology is a license to weave (oops, spin) the yarn we want.

REFERENCES

Hacking, I. *The Social Construction of What?* Cambridge, Mass.: Harvard University Press, 1999.

Harris, R. *Librarianship: The Erosion of a Woman's Profession.* Norwood, N.J.: Ablex, 1992.

Harris, R. "Service Undermined by Technology: Gender Relations, Economics, and Ideology." *Progressive Librarian* 10/11 (1995/96): 13.

Pritchard, S. "Backlash, Backwater, or Back to the Drawing Board." *Wilson Library Bulletin* (June 1994): 42–46.

Schneider, K. G. "Four Librarians of the Apocalypse; Or, What Part of the Paradigm Don't You Understand?" *Wilson Library Bulletin* (October 1994): 35–38.

ANGRY AMAZONS

Library Journal *declined to publish this piece, reasoning as follows: "You [Cronin] had your shot, they [the Amazons] had theirs."*

Mea cupla, mea maxima culpa. I misspelled Hope Olson's name throughout my "Amazons R Us" column (*LJ* [October 15, 2001]: 54) and also, inexcusably, misattributed Karen Schneider's "Amazons with laptops" quotation to Sarah Pritchard. For both of these errors, which rankled greatly in some quarters, I apologize unreservedly. I was also taken to task for citing an out-of-date (ALA) website for Ms. Pritchard's works, although in this case my intention was simply to show that her writings had the de facto seal of approval of the American Library Association. Readers interested in a more comprehensive inventory of Ms. Pritchard's professional writings may thus like to visit her personal website at www.library.ucsb.edu/people /pritchard. I can't say fairer than that, can I?

These gaffes, of course, merely added fuel to the thesaurus-propelled fire of my predominantly female critics ("sad spectacle," "stumbling rant," "sexism," "tumid ritornello," "insipid piece of dreck," "drivel," "prosaic, trite, fatuous, pissy little whine," "reactionary professor," "public misbehavior") which this "Son of Shibboleth" column (see Blaise Cronin, "Shibboleth and Substance in North American Library and Information Science Education") provoked in the December 2001 and January 2002 letters to *Library Journal* and also in other places.

In fact, for a most revealing glimpse into the mind-set of one's critics, and the shrillness of their subterranean objurgations, why don't you check out the online archives of the ALA Feminist Task Force Discussion List (FEMINIST) for the period October 18–December 5, 2001, where most of the comments I've quoted above were originally spawned. This will provide an instructive insight into the way the

Amazons marshaled their forces and thoughts. More generally, it makes clear the potential of the Internet and the Web to mobilize like-minded thinkers. This, of course, can be a powerful force for good, as in the case of so-called suck sites that expose social or corporate injustice. On the other hand, the desire to consort (virtually) with individuals of similar outlook can result in loss of tolerance for alternative perspectives and foster narrow orthodoxies. In his book, *republic.com*, Cass Sunstein argues that the Internet can create "group polarization" (70) and "a balkanized speech market" (84). The FEMINIST listserv certainly bears out his point, at least as far as the present topic is concerned.

The archive contains some absolute zingers, including this gem from Mark Rosenzweig, *Progressive Librarian* editor: "He's boring, he retreads himself, he's looking for attention. He's SO obvious . . . loookatme . . . lookatme . . . lookat me . . . I HAVE A PENIS so I can say anything . . . and LJ will print it ex-cathedra. Probably pees on his foot . . . written by someone who needs Viagra." What one's private parts and bodily functions have to do with one's public utterances remains something of a puzzle, but Mr. Rosenzweig is not alone in his fixation on size. Kathleen de la Peña McCook, of the University of South Florida, for example, spoke of a "little man" with "his little editorship" (a reference, I presume, to the *Annual Review of Information Science and Technology*, which I edit), who uses "a little altar boy Latin" (see above for evidence of this deviant tendency). And so it continued, a pantomime of semipublic pettishness. Not quite "fighting words" in a First Amendment sense, perhaps, but the kind of locker-room speech one doesn't usually associate with either academics or professional librarians.

That said, I can well understand that some FEMINIST subscribers may disagree with and even take exception to my comments, but surely robust argumentation, not ad hominem invective, is the answer. Or is it that the norms of academic debate and dialogic democracy—values that card-carrying ALA members trumpet loudly and persistently—do not apply on this particular listserv? It's all so deliciously ironic in that research, including that of my colleague, Susan Herring, whom I invoked in the original offending column, has apparently documented gender differences in a variety of online communication contexts; as a general rule, women are more likely to avoid confrontation, profanity, and abuse in electronic fora. In the light of the foregoing, it's high time someone turned the research spotlight on FEMINIST. Men may be from Mars (something we hear with numbing regularity these days), but not all female FEMINIST contributors are from Venus, that's for sure.

As if all that wasn't enough, I was taught an important, final lesson via e-mail: Yarn is spun, not woven as I sloppily stated. For that correction, I am most grateful to a member of the (wait for it!) ALA Ad Hoc Quilters Task Force. Perhaps what is really needed, though, in Libraryland is an ALA Ad Hoc Viagra Users Group with yours truly as honorary chairman.

REFERENCES

Cronin, B. "Shibboleth and Substance in North American Library and Information Science Education." *Libri* 45, no. 1 (1995): 45–63.

Sunstein, C. *republic.com*. Princeton, N.J.: Princeton University Press, 2001.

MARGARET RUFSVOLD, PIONEER

Originally published April 2002

I sometimes jog with Katharine Sharp. Which is to say I wear a T-shirt emblazoned with the black-and-white image of the founder of the University of Illinois Graduate School of Library and Information Science. Without the pioneering efforts of Miss Sharp and other early female innovators, I probably would be plying a different trade—no disrespect to Mr. Dewey and his colleagues at Columbia. I certainly wouldn't be writing this column. More specifically, I owe a debt to another farsighted lady, the late Margaret Rufsvold, who almost single-handedly brought Indiana University's (IU) School of Library and Information Science (SLIS) into being.

Miss Rufsvold and I met twice. The exchanges were polite if, inevitably, superficial; she was already in her eighties and slightly infirm. At that time, Miss Rufsvold spent only part of the year in Bloomington, yet she was a constant presence. A portrait hangs in the SLIS library, and the Rufsvold Fund, a permanent endowment, provides generous support annually to doctoral students. Margaret Rufsvold died some months ago. A long-standing connection with our collective past has been broken after many years. Miss Rufsvold joined the Indiana University faculty in 1938, a decade before I was even a twinkle in my parents' eyes. When she retired as dean of the Indiana University Graduate Library School in 1972, I still hadn't earned my MLS (Master of Library Science).

Today, we watch as library science programs in North America and elsewhere metamorphose into generic information studies schools, trading autonomy and identity for a more robust resource base. It's neither surprising nor, in any meaningful sense, regrettable; rather it is an inescapable fact of the evolutionary dynamics of academic life. It is ironic, however, as Miss Rufsvold is doubtless musing from the grave, given her contributions to the formation of this field. As far as I can tell, the first tentative steps at in-house training of librarians at IU began in 1899, though institutionalization of these efforts took some time. In fact, it was not until 1947 that the Division of Library Science was established under Miss Rufsvold's direction within the School of Education. With her very much at the helm, the division eventually emerged from the School of Education and became the Graduate Library School in 1966, which name it retained until 1980 when the present title was adopted. How things have changed. For example, the route followed by Miss Rufsvold in the 1940s is the reverse of that chosen a few years ago by the University of California at Los Angeles (UCLA) for its erstwhile LIS program, which has since been folded into the UCLA School of Education. Two steps forward, one step back seems to be the experience in Libraryland.

It's all too easy to downplay the achievements of one's predecessors. Library science back then was strongly vocational in character and didn't have the research base we take for granted today (*pace* Pierce Butler and Jesse Shera). It was all really rather amateurish, if well intentioned. Formal grounding in theory and research methods and the attendant emphasis on scholarly production were not defining features of the embryonic domain. Miss Rufsvold came to IU with a master's degree in librarianship and relevant real-world experience. To be blunt, we probably wouldn't hire her today, but without her groundbreaking efforts we wouldn't be hiring at all today. There's more to this woman than meets the eye, as I've been discovering. Rummaging through the SLIS archives, I found a few facts worthy of mention. In academic year 1971–72, Miss Rufsvold chaired ten doctoral committees and served as a member of eighteen others. That's pretty impressive, by any standard; indeed, it's more than the collective effort of some contemporary faculties.

When she wasn't administering, teaching, writing, or guiding research, Rufsvold was busy on both the national and international stage, raising the profile of her program and the profession. At home, she was, amongst other things, a consultant to the Office of Education in Washington, D.C., and overseas, a consultant on library services to the College of Education in Bangkok, Thailand. Her legacy is visible well beyond the confines of IU: generations of teachers and administrators around the globe would not be where they are today but for her dedication and effort. She may have honed her skills in the cornfields of the Midwest, but she had, to use that overused word, vision. And, unlike some so-called visionaries, she successfully translated her goals and convictions into tangible and enduring accomplishments. She didn't, in the slightly mangled words of an anonymous alumnus, "spend her time on hypothetical platform making announcements."

Apparently she was an inspiring teacher, judging by the enthusiastic testimonials provided by former students. Here's a description of Miss Rufsvold as a classroom teacher, penned by a well-known (but nameless) professor of library science, then a doctoral student at IU: "She was . . . a strikingly handsome woman, who embodied a kind of energy that was at once recognized and respected by those who encountered her. . . . I marveled at the brilliant way in which the content of her lecture was so effortlessly welded into a coherent whole—she had no notes." I can vouchsafe for part of this encomium: the photographs in our files confirm that she was indeed a striking individual. In every respect, Miss Rufsvold belied the popular occupational stereotype that continues, regrettably, to bedevil the profession.

OF BOOKS AND BOTTLES

The solitary scholar poring over dusty volumes in a wood-paneled, neogothic library constitutes a powerful and enduringly appealing image of the academic calling. In older British universities, there is still a promoted rank—reader—not to be found in this country, as far as I am aware, which is a way station between associate and full professor. The implication is clear: Only the thoroughly well read shall proceed to profess ex cathedra. The centrality of reading was—perhaps still is, in isolated institutions—signaled in other ways via the vocabulary of academia. As undergraduates, we went up to university to *read* classics, natural philosophy, or whatever. Any other phrasing was quite simply *infra dignitatem*. We didn't *do* mathematics or *study* modern languages. We read mathematics or. . . . But so much for the past.

I read, therefore I am—as is the case for so many of one's colleagues in the World of Learning. The bulk of my working and waking hours are devoted to reading. My reading fuels my writing. I read out of necessity, but also for edification and pleasure, though it's sometimes hard to know where the dividing line should be drawn. In fact, so much of what I read, whether properly labeled as recreational or professionally marginal, manages to seep beneficially into the work zone. Nothing, I venture to say, is ever wasted; nothing I read can't serve some professional purpose, even if it amounts to no more than a stylistic bauble or strategically placed *aperçu* in a forthcoming paper or presentation. Of course, such justification constitutes a convenient carte blanche for the promiscuous reader or professional layabout.

Maslow was on the mark when it came to motivation. As with eating, there are two kinds of reading: functional and enriching. A Big Mac on the run serves a purpose (suppression of hunger), but the experience is a million miles from a relaxed *dîner à deux* at La Tour d'Argent complemented by a *grand cru classé* of noble vintage. Food is consumed in both cases, but that's where the similarities end; in the latter, the food, exquisite though it will likely be, is but a part of a much richer experience involving ambience, history, haute cuisine, sociability, and oenology.

Much of my work-a-day reading is necessarily Big Mac-ish in character, but there are still just about enough à la carte experiences to satisfy the soul. Increasingly, those Big Mac moments involve electronic journals, digital libraries, e-books, and myriad Web resources. Wonderfully efficient, and occasionally liberating tools, to be sure, but scarcely what Birkets (1994, 15) had in mind when he talked about the "reading sensibility."

For me, and for many others, I suspect, there is reading and reading. Corny though it may sound, I like books as objects, even if they don't have tooled bindings and gilt lettering. Their physical form and features (whether bland or beautiful) are constitutive of the reading experience. Of course, I can sometimes read the very same words off a screen, and learn as little or as much, but the experience is not the same. The materiality of reading matters. But all this has been said before and nowhere better than in Alberto Manguel's (1996) enchanting book, *A History of Reading*. At one point (258), he mentions the Spanish writer Dámaso Alonso's distaste for public readings because "culture is slowness." How many times while sitting at my desk, in the office, or at home have I lifted my eyes from the page, toyed with the book, glanced around at my surroundings, mulled over the last sentence, paragraph, or chapter, and mused not only on the passing words but on the act of reading itself? The book is the quintessential "convivial" technology, to borrow Ivan Illich's epithet, as far as reading is concerned, for it accommodates reflection and slowness, virtues little valued by postmodernists or geeks.

In an age of fast food, Beaujolais Nouveau, and (Internet) warp time—or what George Steiner (1997, 166) calls "American time"—there's something to be said for measuredness, as proponents of the Slow Food, and now, too, the Slow Cities, movement clearly appreciate (see www.slowfood.com/). A $15 bottle of Beaujolais may be fun to quaff and may, indeed, help break the social ice, but, ultimately, how much more satisfying to anticipate the decanting of a fine claret which has aged sedately for twenty years in the cellar, the imminent discussion of the château's history and vintages, and the shared pleasure to be had from intelligent tasting. As with the book, so with the vine. Every time I uncork a halfway decent bottle from the Mèdoc, I think back to days spent bicycling through the understatedly elegant vineyards of Bordeaux; of the neoclassical splendor of Château Margaux, the fairytale beauty of Pichon-Longueville. . . . I recall the sights, sounds and smells of the region. And maybe to top it all off I pull down from the shelf a copy of *Vivre la Vigne*, Baron Philippe de Rothschild's literary love affair with *le terroir* (Philippe 1981). In a word, I am transported.

Opening the wine opens the memory bank. The bottle, like the book, is a passport to a wider "shadow life" (Birkets 1994, 96). If all I want is a chunk of text, I can go online to Project Gutenberg's website (http://promo.net/pg/); if all I want is an infusion of alcohol, I can take a shot of bourbon. For a more satisfying experience, though, I'll stick with my books and bottles of Bordeaux.

REFERENCES

Birkets, S. *The Gutenberg Elegies: The Fate of Reading in an Electronic Age*. New York: Ballantine Books, 1994.

Manguel, A. *A History of Reading*. London: Flamingo, 1996.

Philippe, B. P. *Vivre la Vigne: Du Ghetto de Francfort à Mouton Rothschild 1744–1981*. Paris: Presses de la Cité, 1981.

Steiner, G. *Errata: An Examined Life*. New Haven, Conn.: Yale University Press, 1997.

Milquetoast and Cookies

Originally published May 2002

Among the more risible neologisms of recent years is "caregiver." It virtually elevates caring for a friend or loved one to a paraprofessional activity, instead of something most of us do naturally most of the time. I tell you, before long there'll be a National Council of Caregivers, with its own journal, annual conference, and all the accoutrements of professionalism. It won't surprise you to learn that I bracket caregiving with nurturing, and in our own little world "nurturing" is a big deal. Variants on the n-word are metastasizing all over the landscape of Libraryland. And it's a not a pretty sight, as I've intimated previously in these pages (see "Amazons R Us").

Let's start with the basics. Librarians are librarians; they are not caregivers, nurturers, social workers, surrogate parents, welfare agents, or therapists. When all is said and done, their role is straightforward: they gather stuff, impose some order on said stuff, and make the stuff available to the public at large. Some specialist skills are brought to bear on the organization of the stuff, along with, one presumes, a modicum of sensitivity to the needs and wants of the patron. Nowhere in this stripped-down occupational brief do notions of nurture intrude. Nor should they. Nurturing and caring are not constitutive of librarianship, and should be left to those with the requisite training . . . and willingness to face the occasional liability suit.

Not long ago, I was reading a performance review of a library director, in which there was explicit concern that the administrator in question was not doing enough "to nurture the staff." Later, in the same document, there was a plangent lament that the organization was not "a joy to work in" for some of the staff. I don't know about you, but I come to work every day to get a job done, not to seek nurture or joy. Joy was not mentioned in my job description, nor prom-

ised during my recruitment. The fact that I rather enjoy my work is a
considerable plus, but it's not a perquisite. Many of you probably
read magazines like *Fast Company* and (the recently deceased) *Industry Standard,* and are familiar with the breezy and sometimes touchy-feely language of twenty-first-century human resources management. Some of it seems eminently sensible; some a little thin on
specifics. Nonetheless, in the age of the postbureaucratic enterprise,
most of us realize that organizational culture and leadership styles
can make a measurable difference to both individual and collective
performance. Although the ineffable may, indeed, matter, that's no
excuse to promote twaddle about joy and nurturing, or rhapsodize
woolly headedly about the feminine qualities of the profession. Ironically, this near-metaphysical language is rooted in certain very concrete (and calorific) practices beloved of Librarylanders.

Every semester in our school, members of the American Library
Association's (ALA) student chapter hold what is termed a "bake
sale," designed to raise much-needed funds to support student activities. I've been known to disparage these activities (though not, I
hasten to add, the underlying goal) as part of the "milk and cookies"
syndrome I associate with the profession. Surely, I'll say to my
blanching colleagues, there are more imaginative, inspiring, effective, and image-enhancing ways to raising a few bucks . . . like a
pay-per-view auto-da-fé of a certain *LJ* columnist? I may be wrong,
but graduate students (and note the word "graduate" here) in other
professional programs, like law, business or journalism, don't seem
to fall into what I'll term the "tea cosy" trap, the way some of our
students and professional colleagues do.

The current president of the ALA, Mitch Freedman, is on record as
saying that librarians' pay will be one of the key issues of his tenure.
The factors that influence public perceptions of status, and by extension, remuneration levels are many and complex. But professional image is an important variable in the mix. Many years ago, I
shared an office in London with an Australian market researcher,
Margaret Slater, who wrote a book entitled *Career Patterns and the
Occupational Image,* published by Aslib in 1979. It's a revealing, if
slightly dated, insight into how the world sees us vis-à-vis other occupational groups. In sum, image matters. So, if we would like to be
valued more highly (and receive tangible expressions of that value
in our paychecks), it might make sense for Mr. Freedman and others
within the ranks of the ALA to examine the signals we send out to

the wider world, particularly the ways in which we seek to valorize nurturing and caregiving as part of the praxis of modern librarianship.

The trend I'm sketching is not altogether new. I have a vague recollection of a stunt carried out in a public library somewhere in this county to hug patrons as they entered the library. Apparently, it was felt that random hugging would work wonders for the library's public image. This kind of nonsense sets the profession back years, and does nothing to advance Mr. Freedman's well-meaning agenda. What I want from a professional, be he or she a lawyer, librarian, or liposuctionist, is competent, ethical, and courteous service. Hugging, nurturing, and caregiving are strictly off limits.

THE UNIVERSITY PRESS

Originally published March 2002

Tomes for tenure. That, I suspect, is the context in which many of us think of university presses. We believe that the university press exists to bring forth worthy scholarship of decidedly limited commercial appeal. The publication of specialized monographs is culturally laudable in its own right, but for many scholars, humanists in particular, the university press performs an essential role in ensuring that they are able to publish the necessary magnum opus upon which tenure in many disciplines still depends. The university press is thus more than a publisher; it is an integral part of the academic reward system. Without university presses, many junior scholars' careers would come to a sticky and premature end. As the Association of American University Presses likes to put it, "University presses do things that wouldn't otherwise get done."

The university press has been around for a long time. The granddaddy of them all is the venerable Cambridge University Press (CUP), founded on a royal charter granted to the university by Henry VIII in 1534. The CUP published its first book about 420 years ago, and since then it has produced works by John Milton, Isaac Newton, Ernest Rutherford, Albert Einstein, and Umberto Eco, to name but a handful. Today, it publishes 2,000 books a year, sold in 200 countries. But the CUP is certainly not typical of the species. Most presses are relatively modest concerns, struggling in many cases to avoid deficits from one year to the next. They operate in, or at the edges of, academe, yet have to deal with the vicissitudes of the commercial marketplace. In a way, they are neither fish nor fowl, and recent developments in online publishing and digital bookselling merely underscore the challenges facing this genteel community.

In this country, there are about ninety university presses. The pioneers (e.g., Johns Hopkins, Chicago) were established in the nineteenth century, with several Ivy League schools following their example early in the twentieth century. Some function on a solid financial footing, thanks either to featherbedding endowments or generous subsidies from their institutional parents. Others are less fortunate, and may be forced to take bold steps to stay afloat. A year or two ago, Iowa State University (ISU) Press, with the blessing of the university trustees, shed its nonprofit status and merged its operations with a U.K. commercial publisher, Blackwell Science. This Mephistophelean bargain allows Blackwell to license the ISU name on a renewable five-year basis. For its part, the press gets much needed access to an annual income stream from the $2 million dowry delivered by its new partner. It can also veto attempts by the new owner to publish tack under the ISU imprint, so all is not lost.

Other kinds of partnerships and initiatives can be expected—think of HighWire Press at Stanford University. Some will entail closer collaboration with university libraries—a natural on-campus ally, though also a potential competitor as evidenced by the growth of library-based digital production centers. Others will involve partnerships of one kind or another with corporate players. A good example was the agreement between e-book publisher, ebrary, and a slew of university presses, including MIT, Stanford, and Wisconsin. Under the terms of this deal, each of the participating presses will make available hundreds, if not thousands, of titles for distribution to expanded markets via ebrary. As with the earlier Questia Media and other yet-to-be-conceived slam-dunk deals, it's not the particulars that count. What's interesting is the way in which the university press world is beginning to innovate, and explore strategic codevelopment opportunities.

But we should not equate digitization with innovation. Instead, let's look at one or two assumptions underlying academic publishing. Should young professors still be expected to publish books, and must these books typically roll off a university press? Why do we assume that scholarly credentials and academic insight can only be packaged and legitimated in the form of a monograph, be it printed or delivered digitally on demand? There are many forms and genres of scholarly communication—note, I didn't say publication—and it may just be that some of those are more useful and meaningful than having one's *grandes pensées* bound between the covers of a minority-appeal book with an estimated, life-cycle readership of fifty souls. For every Milton and Einstein on CUP's backlist, there are thousands of well-meaning career academics whose works, even if sporting a prestigious imprint, are going to make damp squibs seem exciting. In short, we need to think as much about the nature of scholarly creativity and communication as the processes of packaging and distributing codified knowledge.

Columbia University Press's editor-in-chief, Kate Wittenberg, seems to get it. Writing in the *Chronicle of Higher Education*, she describes how Columbia University Press is trying to create "a venue in which scholars can disseminate their work in different forms and at stages . . . to encourage creative, cutting-edge scholarship that is influenced in positive ways by the form in which it is presented." This doesn't mean abandoning quality and peer review, or dragging university presses gleefully down market. Nor does it mean handing over control to bean counters. It does, however, require a little thinking out of the box, and almost inevitably a relaxing of territorial concerns. University administrators, faculty, librarians, and publishing personnel ought to fashion a common understanding of the changing dynamics of scholarly communication, and work, disinterestedly, to create the conditions to ensure the continuing viability of the university press.

The university press is a civilizing influence, one that has persisted for centuries. It's even been argued that great university presses help make great university presidents (Regier 2002). Given the vertiginous pace of merger and acquisition activity in commercial publishing, it is to be hoped that the idea of the university press will thrive and survive.

REFERENCES

Regier, W. G. "Great University Presses Make Greater Presidents." *The Chronicle of Higher Education* (February 22, 2002): B24.

Wittenberg, K. "Cutting-edge Scholarship and Electronic Publishing." *Chronicle of Higher Education* (June 19, 1998): B6.

LOCUS CLASSICUS

Originally published June 2002

I was an undistinguished undergraduate in a distinguished setting. Trinity College Dublin is a cultural and architectural treasure, founded more than four hundred years ago by Queen Elizabeth I. The walled campus, slap bang in the pulsing center of Dublin, is a place apart. The elegant architecture and symmetry of the university's layout will lift even the most jaded of spirits. History is everywhere, from the neoclassical sweep of the Old Library to the priceless pages of the Book of Kells. As you traverse the smooth cobblestones of Front Square, you are following in the footsteps of some truly eminent figures—George Berkeley, Jonathan Swift, Oscar Wilde, Samuel Beckett—and, of course, armies of American tourists. After spending a few minutes in a place like Trinity, it's hard not to question some of the "virtual university" rhetoric which has attracted so much attention in recent years.

The New World has a few academic jewels of its own. Iconic status belongs to Thomas Jefferson's "academical village" at the University of Virginia, but whether it is Trinity or Virginia, the defining feature of the academical village is that student and professor come together in place and time. I fondly recall one-on-one meetings with my philosophy tutor in his rooms, and the occasional midafternoon glass of sherry or Madeira. That genteel, and, admittedly, rather privileged, world has receded in the face of the economics of mass higher education and, more recently, with the spectacular rise in online, distance, and distributed education.

Vast amounts have been written about online education, and many more words will be spilled before we've got a good handle on the subject. I first researched the topic sixteen years ago, and recently had occasion to revisit it when I spent a year as director of Distance Education Planning for Indiana University. That assignment forced me to do my homework. I immersed myself in the available literature—scholarly, futurist, and popular. I analyzed the players, strategies, business models, technologies, and pedagogic claims. And I quickly learned that online education means different things to different people at different times.

First, let's get rid of the notion that it's a case of A or B: old fashioned, face-to-face education versus distributed, virtual learning (Cronin and Crawford 1998). Online education is a multifaceted beast, and should not be viewed as a monolithic construct. A and B are complementary, not oppositional modes of education. Second, Real U is not going to be replaced any time soon by Virtual U. There are several good reasons why: 1) Real U offers a powerful, established brand, and brand matters enormously in the marketplace; 2) Real U (a.k.a. Lifestyle U: see Hal Cohen, *The Industry Standard*) looks after our kids during those highly combustible, late teen years, so there is an abiding demand for these manicured reservations where mischief can be contained and social skills marginally honed; 3) on the whole, Real U does what it does very well (and the best of U.S. higher education is the best there is in the world), and, in any case, is increasingly alert to the challenges and opportunities of e-learning. That is to say, Real U will intelligently combine traditional and avant-garde means of reaching and teaching its students, synchronously and asynchronously; 4) Real U was around a couple of hundred years ago, and probably will still be around a few generations from now, so that piece of framed parchment on your wall bears a meaningful and persistent name. Question: would you want invest in a qualification from a start-up, virtual U which might be taken over five years down the road, so that you end up with an "orphan" degree from an institution which no longer exists? 5) despite the flood of new entrants (from Phoenix to UNext) into the distance/online education marketplace, some of the most significant experimentation and investment is coming from leading Ivies, who see brand and market extension opportunities on the horizon.

If we think of online education more in terms of lifelong learning, a slightly different picture emerges. Here we're talking about an additional market opportunity for which new educational technologies may provide otherwise unachievable solutions. Put Real U to one side, and consider the likely future demand in the workplace for skills renewal and knowledge augmentation. How will society satisfy this net increase in demand for perpetual learning? Is this really the bailiwick of Real U, or do we need a new breed of entrepreneur-ial provider to ensure that the nation's intellectual capital base is regularly refreshed? Think, too, of all those individuals who, whether for domestic or work-related reasons, are currently unable to partake of Real U's traditionally packaged offerings (degrees, cer-tificates, courses), but who can be accommodated by Virtual U's flexible, self-paced, customized offerings delivered electronically via the Web.

For many, the University of Phoenix is the poster child of distance education provision. It attracts tens of thousands of students, mostly in the areas of business administration and management, who take courses both in face-to-face and online mode. Phoenix meets a felt need, is an accredited institution, and has developed a successful business model. It's also a favorite of Wall Street analysts: Phoenix's parent, the Apollo Group, is listed on the stock market. However, Phoenix is not, and should not aspire to be, Real U. For traditional educational providers, place, in the physical sense of the term (think Ionic columns, domed libraries, junior common rooms) is a big part of the package. Indeed, it is a continuing source of comparative ad-vantage.

REFERENCES

Cohen, H. "The Industry Standard." *The Industry Standard* (June 25, 2001): 70–72.

Cronin, B., and H. Crawford. "Letter from America (Pipe Dreams)." *International Journal of Information Management* 18, no. 6 (1998): 461–64.

THE JOYS OF JESSE

I am a member of that despised species, the listserv lurker. Unseen and unheard; leeching and sneering, "listening" and (sometimes) learning. One up from a Peeping Tom on the evolutionary scale, I suppose. It's the classic form of cyber selfishness. Fortunately, economists have a less disparaging name for people like me—free-riders (the academic first cousins of freeloaders). We're the ones who coattail on others' inputs and efforts, contributing nothing to the common pool. On very, very rare occasions, I do react to postings, but invariably it's a back channel response to the sender rather than a reply to the listserv. Put it down to Anglo-Irish reserve.

Don't get me wrong; listservs are occasionally effective, and sometimes efficient, communication channels. They enable scholars and practitioners to stay abreast of developments both inside and well beyond their primary domains of action. They plug us rapidly into breaking news and alert us to imminent trends. Of course, the signal to noise ratio is not quite what one would want: for every genuinely useful message there are ___ (fill in the blank) postings designed to make us ask why we don't simply unsubscribe.

For several years, I have been on JESSE, the open library and information science education forum. I *may* have posted one message in that time, but I really can't recall. Traffic on JESSE is erratic; periods of inactivity followed by staccato postings, followed by a flurry of exchanges, followed by a relapse into near silence (for a sense of this, go to the archive, which is available at www.listserv.utk.edu /archives/jesse.html). The cyclicity may vary, but you get the general picture. Moreover, one can almost always predict whether or not an initial query or statement will provoke an extended (by JESSE standards) exchange. In both these regards, I venture to say that JESSE is not atypical of the medium.

What has struck me most about JESSE, however, is the relationship between topic triviality and traffic density: the dumber the subject, the greater the volume of chatter. Now, there's nothing wrong
with a little lightweight banter online; it's no different from jawbon-
ing around the water cooler: it takes our mind off things and rein-
forces sociability in the workplace. But sometimes JESSEites seem to
lose their marbles. Let me give you an example from February 2002.
The most discussed topic that month was not digital libraries, nor
LIS education, nor even the CIPA (Children's Internet Protection
Act); it was . . . you've guessed it, the "hot librarian."

It all began innocuously enough with a posting alerting us to a
display advertisement in the February 18 issue of *Time* magazine, in
which the Honda Accord V-6 coupe is described as the "automotive
equivalent of a really hot librarian. Good looking, yet intelligent.
Fun yet sophisticated." On reading this, I immediately said to one of
my colleagues, "JESSE's about to light up." Which JESSE duly did,
with zingers coming from all corners of the globe. Trust a hot librarian to get the professorate away from its dusty tomes. One could almost have written the script. A few early respondents remarked on
other ad campaigns that had played off the gendered stereotype. We
learned that Morgan's Spiced Rum had used the tagline "Librarians
by day, Spiced by night" in the United Kingdom, while Bacardi had
plumped for "Librarian by day, Bacardi by night" in the United
States. Old timers reminisced about the Smirnoff ad featuring a
comely wench, which, apparently, had a caption line something like:
"I was the mainstay of the public library, until I discovered
Smirnoff."

Here, perhaps, was an opportunity for JESSE to revisit professional stereotyping and debate the semiotics of display advertising,
but it was not to be. The discussion veered off track and degenerated
into a self-consciously humorous exchange on what the real automotive equivalent of a "hot librarian" ought to be—shades of Stanley Fish's (1994) "The Unbearable Ugliness of Volvos." Forget the
Honda, seemed to be the consensus. A posting from Indiana (not I,
you understand) provided a clear specification: "a lipstick red
longbed pickup truck with duallys, a winch, and a tow package." I
should have known, but then I've been living in Indiana for only
eleven years and I haven't the foggiest idea what a dually is. Some
chap from New Zealand seemed to think the automotive analogue
would necessarily be a Ferrari, but he was soon put in his box by an-

other aficionado of trucks (from Alabama, this time) who felt the original specification was right on the mark—provided a "matching gun rack" was included.

And so it went on until the big end dropped out of the banter. JESSE is now drawing its collective breath, and we, the lurking scum of cyberspace, can hardly wait for the next eruption.

REFERENCE

Fish, S. "The Unbearable Ugliness of Volvos." In *There's No Such Thing as Free Speech,* 273–79. New York: Oxford University Press, 1994.

WELCOME TO MY WEB WORLD

Originally published September 2002

To be is to be seen. And where better than on the Web? One would expect library and information science (LIS) programs to have a significant and compelling Web presence. After all, these are important production sites for future Web masters, information architects, and usability testers. My starting point was the list of websites for accredited programs on the ALISE (Association for Library and Information Science Education) homepage. Oddly, Clark Atlanta, Clarion, and the University of Puerto Rico don't provide hyperlinks, though I did eventually find homepages for the first two. Perhaps this trio is unusually shy, or they have no real story to tell. I'll leave it to others to rank systematically the quality of different sites in terms of cognitive ergonomics; my tour was superficial and impressionistic. I looked at what the schools had to say about themselves (identity performance, to use the posh term) as if I were the proverbial (and politically incorrect) man from Mars.

Some sites are threadbare; some information rich. A few have immediate design appeal; most are look-alikes. Overall, I'm not sure that we practice what we preach in our Web design courses with great conviction. For me, one school stands head and shoulders above the rest of the pack. And, no, it's not Indiana, though, naturally, it comes close. Michigan's School of Information's Web page is swaggeringly self-confident in terms of effect and content. That's not to say that design/usability guru Jakob Nielsen would give it his blessing, but the impression one takes away is of a pulsing and well-resourced program. Michigan's sponsored research expenditures for fiscal 2000 were more than $6 million, the site graphically and proudly asserts. One also gets a sense of a school that's intellectually alive and extremely well-connected to the movers and shakers in the larger information world. Were I a student, I'd be sorely tempted, Michigan winters notwithstanding.

Down Texas way, a different picture emerges. The unsuspecting visitor to the LIS program at the University of Texas at Austin is greeted by an image that is unlikely to fade rapidly: three beaming ladies, former or current faculty members, standing with their index fingers and pinkies pointing out and upwards. This, apparently, signifies "Hook 'em Horns!" The cultural (not to mention professional) significance of the gesture was lost on me, but it said something about that school. Rambling about Pittsburgh's luridly labeled homepage (canary yellow dominates its logo), I decided for no good reason to look at the photographs from the 1997 (yes, 1997) Board of Visitors reception, but was told in each case "Sorry, that file doesn't exist." Surely, the School of Information Sciences can do better than that. Disgruntled, I headed off to North Carolina Central University where I was welcomed by something straight out of Eric Segal's *Love Story*. "No bird soars too high if he soars with his own wings." The similarity between some homepages and Hallmark greeting cards is increasingly hard to miss. The visitor to the University of Missouri's School of Information Science & Learning Technologies is told that the program is "creating and exploring the intersection of information and learning"—whatever that may mean. But things get worse. At Arizona, the school's vision is trumpeted on its homepage: "To serve as a catalyst to enhance the conduits between information and society." This mangled metaphor foregrounds the container schema, long considered passé in certain circles of Libraryland. I was sorely tempted to entitle this column "Catalysts and Conduits."

Catchphrases are in. I should know: I came up with Indiana's rather fey "Making information make a difference." Some are more banal than others, and most are uninspiring. The University of Southern Mississippi announces that "the future is online and so is SLIS" while up in the wilds of Alberta the come-on line is: "Understanding information; exploring issues, creating access, pursuing equity." Nothing if not ambitious. According to the dean of Toronto's Faculty of Information Studies, there's "never been a better time to be an information professional," provided students can both "reinvent" themselves and "articulate and parlay their considerable professional competencies . . . into a variety of emerging job markets." It sounds painful, but no doubt it's a recipe for success. Similar enthusiasm, predictably, is in evidence in La La Land. The UCLA Web page announces authoritatively that "over half the nation's work-force is now directly engaged in producing, processing, and distrib-uting information" and that "information professionals are in un-precedented demand." And where better to stake out one's claim than in Southern California: "This is really paradise," we're told. Leaving paradise, I clicked my way up to Seattle via the Midwest, where the faculty at the University of Illinois have laid out their views on the Chief Illiniwek symbol. Our man from Mars is told in no uncertain terms that the chief's time has passed and that his con-tinuing existence "directly hinders each aspect of the GSLIS mis-sion." A feather in their collective cap, so to speak.

The enthusiasm for the new at the University of Washington is in-fectious, and the recently rebaptized Information School proudly de-clares on its Web page that they "are working hard to make the iSchool one of the top information schools in the world." One ex-pects a little boosterism in homepages, but at times the chutzpah is hard to stomach. The director of the relatively small library school at the University of British Columbia not only lauds the "exceptional research productivity of his faculty," but goes on to describe UBC as "one of the best universities in the world." Quite!

In short, all our schools are innovative, productive, highly ranked, forward-looking, and professionally engaged. At least, that's what we'd like the man from Mars to believe. However, an hour or two spent surfing ALISE member websites would soon disabuse our ex-traplanetary friend, I can assure you, unless (as I suspect may well be the case) they've all changed beyond recognition since I wrote this piece.

THE KNOWLEDGE MANAGEMENT DRUG

Originally published 2001

Knowledge management (KM) is sometimes marketed like a performance-enhancing drug. The professional literature abounds with recipes and prescriptions for organizational renewal. There is broad agreement on some of the steps involved: build up the intellectual capital base, reengineer core business processes, share know-how, and exploit existing knowledge stocks. It may not be as easy as popping pills, but trust the consultants and follow the instructions, and the benefits of organizational pharmacotherapy will surely flow.

In reality, things are not so simple. Organizations exhibit very different personalities and metabolic rates. Work-group members may share emotions and moods and the groups can even take on psychological lives of their own. Thus, what works in one context may not work in another. The linear logic and mechanistic instruments proposed by many consulting firms take little account of the nuanced nature of organizational life or the quiddities of human behavior—nothing new in that, of course. Clearly, organizations have different goals, social contexts, histories, value systems, and reward structures. Such factors can have a significant effect on how ICTs (information and communication technologies) are configured and used in different settings. In short, organizational culture will have a direct bearing on whether the KM pill produces the desired outcomes, unintended side effects, or, in extreme cases, iatrogenic dysfunction.

Organizational culture is a slithery construct, difficult to operationalize. While we may not be able to define it with ease, we know it when we see it: the youthful frenzy of a dotcom is different from the buttoned-down culture of an old-line *Fortune* 500 corporation, which, in turn, is rather different from the rhythms of academic life at an Ivy League institution. And without too much formal training, we can distinguish between the organizational systems and structures associated with different leadership styles, such as elitist-charismatic or functional-traditional. For now, a good working definition of organizational culture has been provided by Schienstock (2000): "a network of interlocking rituals, norms, assumptions, and values that have developed out of continuous interactions among the members of an organisation." Of course, organizational culture is not just of interest to behavioral psychologists and anthropologists. As Schienstock notes, it "influences the meanings and functions attributed to modern ICTs, while the material structures of ICTs shape the emerging organisation culture." In the language of sociotechnical systems analysis, culture and technology are co-constitutive: in everyday language, mutual shaping takes place.

The KM consulting literature is awash with technocentric nostrums, from intranets through knowledge bases to data warehousing and mining, but noticeably deficient in addressing the messy matter of culture. At times, the concept is reified, being treated as something that can be measured and manipulated with precision. In the scholarly literature, the concept, while neither invisible nor quite so trivialized, is still less prominent than one might expect. That said, Nonaka and Konno (1998) identify four categories of organizational knowledge assets: experiential (tacit knowledge shared through common experiences), conceptual (explicit knowledge articulated through images, symbols, and language), systemic (systematized and packaged explicit knowledge) and, lastly, routine (tacit knowledge routinized and embedded in actions and practices). It is in the last of these that organizational culture features, but it is not exactly center stage in their analysis.

On the other hand, Max Boisot's (1999) ambitious book on knowledge management devotes an entire chapter to the idea of culture as a knowledge asset. He describes how different kinds of enterprises—bureaucracies, fiefs, market-based enterprises, and clans—treat knowledge assets, and how the cultural traits associated with these broad categories affect organizational learning, tacit knowledge exchange, and interorganizational transactions. Some of Boisot's hypotheses run contrary to popularly held management beliefs. He argues, for example, that "centripetal cultures block learning whereas centrifugal ones promote it." Such a claim does not sit comfortably with the operating assumptions and social norms that underpin command-and-control or highly bureaucratic organizations.

In many environments, KM is equated with developing knowledge inventories and managing structural intellectual capital—in short, the codification of content and institutionalization of information resources, tangibly embodied in knowledge bases, patent collections, libraries, and such like. This approach may work fine in the business world, but possibly less so in other organizational cultures. In academia, for instance, we are likely to stress knowing over knowledge, process over artifacts, interaction over institutionalization. There is less emphasis on gathering "objective" indicators of successful knowledge capture than on establishing the underlying conditions that foster effective social interaction and creativity. Of course, it is a gross simplification to suggest that conceptions of, and approaches to, KM in the two cultures (corporate and academic) are quite so clear-cut. It is, however, important to recognize that learning occurs in social contexts, and that the sociocognitive characteristics of groups, be they project teams, distributed collaborations, communities of practices, invisible colleges, or specialized disciplinary clusters, will materially shape approaches to knowledge creation, transfer, and utilization. While it may be possible to impose a KM strategy on the managerial hemisphere of the modern university (procurement, estate management, marketing, and similar functions), the mere idea of a turnkey KM strategy being imposed on the academic domain by a business savvy university president is risible.

REFERENCES

Boisot, M. H. *Knowledge Assets: Securing Competitive Advantage in the Information Economy.* Oxford: Oxford University Press, 1999.

Nonaka, I., and N. Konno. "The Concept of 'Ba': Building a Foundation for Knowledge Creation." *California Management Review* 40, no. 3 (1998): 40–54.

Schienstock, G. Towards a Reflexive Organization in the Global Information Economy. *Towards the Learning Society. Innovation and Competence Building with Social Cohesion for Europe.* Quita da Marinha, Guincho, Lisbon, 28–30 May 2000.

INFORMATION WARFARE

Originally published July 2002

David and Goliath is a tale for all times, but perhaps never more so than today. Instead of a sling, information technology is digital David's weapon of choice. The principle of substituting brains for brawn has taken out a new lease on life in the information age, and triggered a torrent of speculation on the nature and significance of what is fashionably termed "asymmetrical conflict." Neologisms, such as cyberwar, network-centric warfare, and neocortical warfare, trip effortlessly off the tongues of military leaders, defense experts, and policy gurus alike, while military historians invoke the initialism RMA (Revolution in Military Affairs) to capture the impact of ICTs (information and communication technologies) on military strategy and the conduct of war. Clearly, something is afoot (Cronin and Crawford 1999).

There are many definitions of the generic term "information warfare," but John Alger's has the virtue of being both widely applicable and mercifully succinct: "Information warfare consists of those actions intended to protect, exploit, corrupt, deny, or destroy information or information resources in order to achieve a significant advantage, objective or victory over an adversary." For more on this and related background, you may like to look at my article "Information Warfare: Peering Inside Pandora's Postmodern Box," which appeared recently in *Library Review*. Today, almost anyone can aspire to be an information warrior; the ability to launch a cyber-attack is much less closely linked to a would-be aggressor's strength or military sophistication than is the case with most forms of conventional warfare. Thus, the theory goes, the United States, being heavily dependent, both militarily and economically, on ICTs, is itself highly vulnerable to information attack. Paradoxically, Goliath's greatest strength is also his greatest weakness. But what, you may be asking yourself, has any of this got to do with you?

The principles of information warfare, as Alger's definition makes clear, can be applied widely, and will very likely have an impact on both our personal and professional lives. Already, the tools and techniques of IW are being adapted for nonmilitary purposes, such as political activism and civil disobedience, and also finding their way into our everyday lives—cyberstalking is a particularly insidious and fast-growing crime, with females being disproportionately targeted. As it happens, I have some firsthand experience of what it's like to be the target of a cybersmear campaign. In the past few years, I've had my e-mail identity spoofed, received anonymous hate mail, and watched, impotently, as professional colleagues worldwide receive occasionally libelous commentary via the Internet. This, regrettably, is now almost commonplace. My own case is quite unimportant, compared with, say, the very public naming of doctors who practice abortion on the infamous Nuremberg Files website (www.christiangallery.com/atrocity/), but at least the experience has helped me better appreciate the underlying attractions (e.g., anonymity, first strike advantage) of information warfare, or personal cyberterrorism, if you will, for the would-be attacker.

The Net is a massive leveler in some respects, eroding established status and power differentials, with results that are both benign and malign. An embittered student or professional colleague can make one's life a misery, if he or she wishes, by cleverly exploiting the communicative capabilities of the Net. On the other hand, the voice of the "little man" can now be heard in ways that make corporate behemoths sit up and take notice. Just think of so-called suck sites that act as magnets for criticisms and complaints against "big business." Fortunately, I've not yet stumbled across blaisecroninsucks.org, but no doubt it's only a matter of time before I, too, get my fifteen minutes of unwanted Warholian fame on the Web.

Information warfare is a topic of growing interest to the corporate sector. The annual cost of cracking and hacking to U.S. business is enormous, according to surveys (www.gocsi.com/prelea_000321 .htm) conducted jointly by the Computer Security Institute and the San Francisco branch of the Federal Bureau of Investigation. The threats range from simple defacing of websites through denial of service to systematic data corruption and theft of proprietary information. Consequently, information security and assurance are major challenges facing businesses and, indeed, organizations of all kinds. Corporate information specialists, systems librarians, and competitive intelligence specialists need to be alert to the threat of cyberattack and knowledgeable about the technical and other means of protecting the information assets under their control from damage by outsiders or "corrupted insiders."

Of course, the threat extends well beyond the world of business. My own institution (Indiana University) attracted considerable, if unwelcome, media attention lately when thousands of graduate students' social security numbers were stolen by a hacker and posted on a public computer site in Sweden. It's not that far-fetched to imagine an individual hacker, or a group of disgruntled (former) employees corrupting online library catalogs or launching a distributed denial of service attack to bring down a library's operations. Such incursions and disruptions may seem relatively trivial (after all, they are not in the same league as degrading or destroying mission- or life-critical information) but for the fact that information on patrons' borrowing practices could easily be compromised.

The social benefits of internetworking are real and enormous. The downsides and dangers, we're beginning to learn, are no less significant. Hackers, crackers, and phreaks are here to stay, be they lone rangers in cyberspace or tightly orchestrated groups operating with strategic intent against a nation-state. We all need to become more aware of the nature of information warfare and cyberterrorism, and, in the process, develop a heightened sense of the technical, social, procedural, and ethical issues associated with computer security. These days, David is never more than a keystroke or two away.

REFERENCES

Cronin, B. "Information Warfare: Peering Inside Pandora's Postmodern Box." *Library Review* 50, no. 5 (2001).

Cronin, B., and H. Crawford. "Information Warfare: Its Application in Military and Civilian Contexts." *The Information Society* 15, no. 4 (1999): 257–63.

POSTSCRIPT TO
INFORMATION WARFARE

This piece is a review of an important book on digital warfare, namely, Gregory J. Rattray's Strategic Warfare in Cyberspace, *published by the MIT Press in 2001. I wrote the review two weeks after the terrorist attacks of September 11, 2001, and I am reprinting it here to serve as a reminder that the kind of threat scenarios sketched in "Information Warfare" do not mean that nondigital attack options have been abandoned by terrorists.*

A favorite cyberwar threat scenario entails the downing of a jetliner either as a result of an enemy attack on the FAA's (Federal Aviation Administration) national air traffic control system or the targeted disruption of a plane's onboard computer and communication systems by a group of terrorists or a hostile foreign power. A great deal has been written in the last decade on both information warfare (opportunistic, tactical, and strategic) and network-centric terrorism, but the frequently apocalyptic scenarios rehearsed in the professional and popular press, of which the sabotaged jetliner is but one example, have yet to occur. Despite the numerous, widely reported incursions of DoD (Department of Defense) and other high-security computer systems and networks by hackers of one kind or another, the much heralded "digital Pearl Harbor"—the rationale for establishing the Critical Information Infrastructure Commission in 1996 by then-President Clinton—has not taken place. As Gregory Rattray, a lieutenant colonel in the U.S. Air Force, notes in this compendious and remarkably level-headed volume, "[t]he actual resiliency of key U.S. information infrastructures in the face of orchestrated, malicious attacks remains unknown" (425). So far, the doomed jetliner scenario—the kind of scenario routinely developed and assessed by RAND consultants and other experts on military and guerrilla strategy—remains just that.

Two weeks ago, however, four American commercial jetliners were hijacked by terrorists and targeted at U.S. assets of high symbolic import. Terrorist experts and military analysts had considered the "flying Molotov cocktail" as a theoretical possibility in their simulations, but few, if any, had envisaged its enactment; fewer still imagined that a group such as al-Qaeda, the prime suspect at the time of writing, could have executed such a plan with such chilling efficiency and spectacular effectiveness. Most terrorism and counterterrorism experts had been assessing strategic information warfare possibilities (e.g., degrading U.S. Air Force logistics support systems) or the threat posed to the U.S. civilian population by weapons of mass destruction (WMDs), such as anthrax or nuclear explosives. To some extent, the military and academic experts were blindsided as a result of their focus on critical vulnerabilities in the nation's digital information infrastructure, and, as a result, the U.S. zone of sanctuary was penetrated for the first time, with massive psychological repercussions. The defense establishment will likely have learned another lesson from the attacks on the World Trade Center towers and the Pentagon, namely, the importance of distinguishing between Internet-based warfare and net terrorism. As John Arquilla and colleagues have repeatedly stressed,

> *netwar* refers to an emerging mode of conflict and crime at societal levels, involving measures short of traditional war, in which the protagonists use network forms of organization and related doctrines, strategies and technologies attuned to the information age. These protagonists are likely to consist of dispersed small groups who communicate, coordinate, and conduct their campaigns in an internetted manner.

The key point here is to distinguish between organizational structure (loosely linked, leadership networks) and the use of computer networks (the Internet) to achieve terrorist objectives.

Strategic Warfare in Cyberspace is a most welcome antidote to the hyperbole and simplifications to be found in much of what is written on the subject of information warfare and the Revolution in Military Affairs (RMA). Rattray's 500-page monograph is cogently written, measured in tone, and very well structured. It is the most comprehensive discussion of asymmetric, information-based warfare that I have come across. The author begins by providing a clear and bounded definition of information warfare, and tracing its origins within U.S. military doctrine during the 1990s. He is critical of the broad definitions used by academics in particular: "Everything from jamming Serbian air defense radars to manipulating Rwandan radio broadcasts to stealing computer-generated plans for Boeing's next airliner has been thrown into the mix" (463). Rattray's definition does not include either kinetic warfare (mechanical attacks on computers and communication networks) or electronic warfare (electromechanical attacks). Also excluded from the analytic frame are information terrorism, perception-based, or epistemological warfare, cyberstalking, computer crime, hacking, and industrial espionage, whether corporate- or state-sponsored. Second, his focus throughout is on actions designed to achieve strategic or political goals: "this book addresses strategic information warfare as a means for state and nonstate actors to achieve objectives through digital attacks on an adversary's centers of gravity" (14). Note the term "centers of gravity," which appears again and again throughout this volume, reminding the reader that the emphasis is on attacking, or defending, critical components of a nation's overall information infrastructure. To make his point, he provides a detailed analysis of the successes and failures of the joint American/British strategic bombing campaign against the Germans in World War II. The point of this analogy is to impress on the reader the four conditions necessary for successfully waging strategic warfare, of whatever kind. These he summarizes as (99–100) offensive freedom of action; significant vulnerability (i.e., centers of gravity) to attack; minimization of prospects for effective retaliation and escalation; and vulnerabilities that can be identified, targeted, and assessed when damaged.

The author provides a detailed description of the U.S. information infrastructure in terms of its openness, interconnectedness, reliance on standardized platforms and protocols, complex public/private sector character, and vulnerability to cascading effects. More particularly, he addresses (222) the subject of human intellectual capital formation: how does the United States develop "a pool of human capital with advanced technological skills to assess and protect large-scale infrastructures in the twenty first century?" He also discusses at length the sociolegal implications of the growing need for more invasive counterintelligence capability in an open society—an issue that the events of September 11, 2001, in New York, Washington, and Pennsylvania have catapulted into public consciousness. The question of skills is important, both for the would-be aggressor and the potential target. It's one thing to assert the ease with which asymmetrical warfare can be initiated (low cost of entry, etc.) but quite another to assemble teams with detailed technical knowledge of the hugely complex variety of legacy, current, and emerging systems to be found in a nation as information systems-dependent as the United States.

But despite the parallels, digital warfare tools are crucially different from conventional weapons for reasons that include the following (468): they diffuse more easily to both state and nonstate actors; they afford greater opportunities for asymmetrical strategies; and they are deployed in cyberspace, an environment not controlled by sovereign governments. It is clear from this somber analysis of America's defensive information warfare strategies and capabilities that the nation is highly vulnerable to attack, even if the worst-case scenarios have yet to unfurl. One of Rattray's recommendations is that the United States should establish a "declaratory deterrence policy" (478) that would make clear to would-be aggressors the scale and kind of response a strategic information attack on U.S. assets or citizens would precipitate. But perhaps the most important lesson to be learned from this book—a lesson learned painfully only two weeks ago—is the role played by intelligence and counterintelligence measures in protecting the civilian infrastructure and ensuring homeland security.

Strategic Warfare in Cyberspace is a sober book that deserves to be read widely and carefully. It is authoritative, copiously referenced, and provides the burgeoning scholarly literature with a much-needed historical perspective on the conduct of strategic warfare. If a revised edition is planned, I would suggest that chapter 4 on the development of U.S. strategic airpower be removed (the lessons described in this section are sketched effectively elsewhere in the text, as it happens) and that chapter 3 on establishing organizational technological capacity be pruned. I also believe that such a lengthy text would benefit from the inclusion of more graphics.

REFERENCE

Arquilla, J., D. Ronfeldt, and M. Zanini. Networks, Netwar, and Information-age Terrorism. In *Countering the New Terrorism*, ed. I. O. Lesser, et al. Santa Monica, Calif.: Rand, 1999. Available online at www.rand.org/publications/MR/MR989/.

DIGIBABBLE

Originally published February 1998

The genie is out of the bottle. Logorrhea rules. Millions of words a minute flood across the Net: scholarly and serious, demotic and daft. Never have so many tongues wagged so waspishly and wittily in warp time. And nowhere more so than in the United States, where digibabble is pandemic. With the advent of the Internet and Web, we are witnessing a paradigmatic shift in how we converse and commune. Old rules and constraints have fallen away. Cyber salons devoted to every imaginable subject (from cryogenics to crypto fascism) have sprouted up to satisfy our need to command disembodied others' attention. Poor Madame de Sévigné must be turning in her grave.

The barriers are down; our inhibitions cast aside. Remember the cartoon: "On the Internet no one knows you're a dog?" Finally, the odious have their podium, to quote John Perry Barlow. In cyberspace all voices are equal and, like Orwellian pigs, we squeal with egalitarian glee at our every posting, rebuttal, and flame. Vanity publishing was an avocation of my great aunt Ethel. Her novels had little literary merit, but they looked the part, so to speak. What we are witnessing today is more appropriately labeled vainglorious publishing, as every Tom, Dick, and Harriet expostulates electronically, with little regard for conventions or couthness.

In the po-mo world of the Net, prosody takes a back seat to persona. It is a reincarnation of the "me" culture of the 1960s. But that will come as no surprise to anyone who is even remotely familiar with American tabloid TV, where the gross and gullible pour out their souls to baying studio audiences and millions of slack-jawed viewers. The volunteer exhibitionism that we have come to associate with daytime TV has migrated to the Net, where the traditionally timid and status-challenged exploit its impersonality to hawk their opinionated banalities to fellow Net denizens. Hurrah for a level playing field, runs the chorus. Beware digital dumbing down, intone the skeptics. George Steiner's prophetic words from *After Babel* come to mind: "The bruit of human voices, so mysteriously diverse and mutually baffling, shuts out the sound of the Logos."

As *Wired* magazine never tires of telling us, we are witnessing the birth of nothing less than digital democracy. But then, we all know what the British public thinks of *Wired*'s agenda. Still, one cannot but be amused as the Mother of All Democracies attempts to transfer the ideals of the Founding Fathers to the information superhighway. Hyde Park Corner on a Sunday afternoon seems painfully anachronistic by comparison, as ideologues of every conceivable hue mount their virtual soapboxes. Incidentally, one of the most popular features on America Online (AOL) is the Buddy List, which lets you know whenever your friends are online—there's nothing like a captive audience. The Web, in particular, is a hospitable environment for the lunatic fringe, notably cultists and conspiracy theorists— think of Heaven's Gate and TWA Flight 800. Here, crazy ideas, like viruses, spread widely and rapidly, their provenance and plausibility unchallenged by uncritical minds. As the *Washington Post* put it so appositely recently, "We live in a time besotted with Bad Information." The Web is set to become the millennial medium of choice for those who have no time for scientific method and forensics. A feeding frenzy of foolishness is imminent.

Electronic agora, combinatorial conversations, and scholarly skywriting have become commonplace in our professional lives. Global networking is profoundly transforming the way we work—enlarging discussion fora, demarginalizing peripheral peers, exposing cant, and pressure cooking new ideas and insights in a way that I could never have imagined as I traversed the cobblestones of Trinity College, Dublin, a stumbling freshman in a real community of scholars. The instrumental benefits of ubiquitous computing are undeniably staggering. But then there's the rest: the inane, the deviant, the dubious. Not to mention the progressive debasement of literary style and epistolary conventions which cyberia promotes. Purists and prescriptivists may weep as consciousness streams, but to little or no avail. Pandora is out of her box.

We celebrate the emergence of virtual communities, yet seem oblivious to the demographics of introversion. What's wrong with a little intersubjective sedimentation . . . with orality? Why spurn social spaces for the world of electrons? Why hide behind the screen, toy with avatars, and juggle multiple identities when we could actually speak face-to-face with our friends and neighbors? Why not go to the piazza or pub (instead of MUDs, MOOs, or electronic simulacra of Jefferson's Academical Village) and be, well, sociable? Whatever the answers, it may be too late: the couch potato has cloned itself in front of the PC, and the slide toward an essentially sedentary and mediated culture now seems irreversible; weight and wiredness are increasingly correlatively on this side of the Atlantic.

Netizens, in their appropriation of the language of community life, appear not to recognize the irony of the situation, while self-anointed digerati merely chide us for adopting fundamentalist and dystopian frames of thinking and for failing to understand the complementarity of media and modes of interaction in the emerging economy of presence. But the social costs of ubiquitous networking (addiction, anomie, displacement) have yet to be calculated. Until then, a little skepticism might not go amiss.

REFERENCE

Steiner, G. *After Babel: Aspects of Language and Translation*. Oxford: OUP, 1992.

DIGIBABBLE MEETS PTOLEMY

"Digibabble" was intended to be a mock-pompous piece, though I am not sure everyone interpreted it thus. At least Ptolemy, the pseudonymous editor of the Association of American Geographers' (AAG) newsletter, seems not to have. "Digibabble" lampoons much of the drivel and quackery that float across the Net, and laments the loss of epistolary style in the face of the rising tide of electronic effluent. In this admittedly arch essay, I offer no research evidence to buttress my cavalier statements, and I'd most likely be up a gum tree if I were seriously challenged to do so.

One of the joys of the Web is the stumble factor. You turn up the most surprising things in the most surprising places. For academics like myself, it can be quite instructive to key in one's name with a commercial search engine and see what is retrieved. I never cease to be amazed by the kinds of references to one's work and ideas that pop up. Intrigued by this phenomenon, I and a number of colleagues conducted a formal investigation of Web-based mentions of well-known information science professors, which was published as "Invoked on the Web" in the *Journal of the American Society for Information Science*. We found that scholars (and their ideas) are being cited, discussed, debated, lauded, and denigrated in a wide variety of places and in many languages. Most of us probably have no idea that our ears should be burning.

Which brings us back to Ptolemy's editorial. I had never seen a copy of the AAG's newsletter and I doubt if I would ever have sought it out. But searching the Web under "Blaise Cronin" I found my article "Digibabble" in the *International Journal of Information Management* co-cited on a syllabus with Ptolemy's editorial, "Digibabble and Better." A playful Ptolemy took me to task for being "more impressed with the Web's disadvantages than with its opportunities." He (she?) chided my pessimism and counterbalanced my negativism with an upbeat review of high-quality library-related websites that help navigate users through the mass of mediocrity. This, of course, is one area in which Libraryland continues to make contributions, OCLC's CORC (Cooperative Online Resource Catalog) project is a notable example of quality control in action. Some may argue that attempts to catalog the Web are as futile as King Canute's efforts to turn back the tide. But that is to miss the point of such undertakings, which is to selectively identify, organize, and make available quality-assured information, for which the Web is an ideal delivery medium. The more organizations like OCLC manage to affix their seals of approval to Web sites, the less users will be distracted by digibabble, less likely to be seduced by snake oil.

But there is another angle to all of this. In an age of 500 cable channels and 5,000,000 websites, the competition for eyeballs and mindshare is fierce. No longer do we all read the same newspaper, listen to the same radio broadcast, or watch the same broadcast news programs. We no longer have, to quote a nameless commentator I heard on a CNN discussion panel, a "unifying uncle" like Walter Cronkite. More and more, we hear what we want to hear, and see what we want to see. There will soon be as many ideologies and viewpoints as there are website owners. In his book, *republic.com*, constitutional law scholar Cass Sunstein considers the dissipative and fractionating effects of the Web and the resultant loss of social solidarity.

> New technologies, emphatically including the Internet, are dramatically increasing people's ability to hear echoes of their own voices and to wall themselves off from others. An important result is the existence of *cybercascades*—processes of information exchange in which a certain fact or point of view becomes widespread, simply because so many people seem to believe it.

Soon, we won't just be bowling alone, to appropriate Robert Putnams' effective metaphor, but blathering and blogging—to use the patois of the hour—alone from our Web-based soapboxes.

REFERENCES

Cronin, B., H. W. Snyder, H. Rosenbaum, A. Martinson, and E. Callahan. "Invoked on the Web." *Journal of the American Society for Information Science* 49, no. 14 (1998): 1319–28.

Sunstein, C. *republic.com.* Princeton, N.J.: Princeton University Press, 2001.

THE LAST RESORT

This isn't a review of the movie of the same name. Nor is it a treatise on destination management in the tourism industry. It's a statement of the obvious about libraries. Every moment of every day we make choices and trade-offs: Homo sapiens as rational actor. We calculate effort against outcomes, costs against benefits, risks against rewards. Sometimes we do it with great deliberation, but often it's instinctive—a gut reaction. Should we drive or fly, take a short cut and risk getting lost or stick to the beaten path, hold out for the perfect solution or plump for a merely satisfactory one, go to the reference library or use the Web? Often the perfectionist in us takes a back seat to the pragmatist. We may not have the time, energy, or necessary information to make a textbook decision, so we suboptimize. It was the Nobel laureate Herb Simon who coined the terms "satisficing behavior" and "bounded rationality" to characterize these aspects of human behavior.

Other scholars have noticed our penchant for minimizing resistance and economizing on effort. George Kingsley Zipf came up with his celebrated "Principle of Least Effort," and Thomas Allen with, if my memory serves me correctly—note this instance of bibliographic sloth, or satisficing behavior, on the part of yours truly—"The 30-Meter Principle," which shows how informal communication between researchers decreases as a function of physical separation. Or, as he put in his much-cited *ARIST* (*Annual Review of Information Science and Technology*) chapter, "communication probability decreases with the square of distance" (11).

Decades worth of public library surveys (of users and, more importantly, nonusers) have taught us a number of things, notably that location and distance have an important bearing upon frequency of use. Simply put, the number of visits falls off as the distance increases. That, of course, is why we have branch libraries, bookmobiles, and (latterly) kiosks. "Build it and they will come" is not a motto that library planners should heed too closely. We also know from the earliest studies of catalog use that patrons can be put off if they don't immediately find what they're looking for. And we also know that'll they'll give up if the library signage and classification systems are inhospitable. Library designers can unwittingly provide the half-hearted or timid user with any number of excuses to become a seriously lapsed user.

Of course, as long as libraries were the principal repositories of print materials, they had the upper hand: either the user invested extra effort or left frustrated. The Internet, Web, Borders, Amazon.com, Barnes and Noble, and such like had yet to appear on the horizon. However, things have changed. The de facto monopoly that libraries exercised (and I'm exaggerating here for effect, it need hardly be said) is being eroded. Ten years ago, the writing of even this little piece would have required at least one or two visits to the library, if only to double-check my Allen, Simon, and Zipf references. And, bear in mind, my office is located in the main university library building. Yet, I refuse to budge, preferring to use Google. Three keystrokes are deemed preferable to a one-minute stroll along the corridor (proof positive of the thirty-meter principle). But this is no longer an isolated instance in my working life, nor am I an isolated statistic within my peer population. And it's not just with to regard to reference queries or bibliographic checking. I and my kind routinely scoop up e-preprints, postings, working papers, and journal articles from cyberspace. Increasingly, the path of least resistance leads to the Web.

Which brings me to Andrew Odlyzko's recent article, "The Rapid Evolution of Scholarly Publishing." This thought-provoking paper, which I naturally downloaded as a pdf file, shows that the dominance of print over electronic is waning. There is a seemingly ineluctable decline in print journal subscriptions of the order of 3–5 percent per year. Meanwhile, server log analyses show that "hit" rates and the number of downloads are growing at the rate of 50–100 percent per year. If, the author asks, these growth rates persist, what sort of future will there be for the traditional scholarly monograph and the printed journal? Odlyzko is not persuaded that scare mongering about loss of quality control and erosion of traditional peer review will be sufficient to hold back the flood.

These developments call into question some of the operating and institutional assumptions underpinning the typical research library. Since we value convenience above almost all else, we will often settle for a good instead of the very best paper on a particular subject, and, increasingly, the Web offers an attractive range of easily accessible "near substitutes" to the journals of record held by academic libraries. As Odlyzko says, "to stay relevant, scholars, publishers, and librarians will have to make even larger efforts to make their material easily accessible." If not, they and we will be bypassed. So, why, you might well ask yourself, am I publishing this in book form rather than posting it on my personal Web page?

REFERENCES

Allen, T. J. Information Needs and Uses. In *Annual Review of Information Science and Technology,* ed. C. A. Cuadra, 3–29. Chicago, Ill.: Encyclopaedia Britannica, 1969.

Odlyzko, A. M. "The Rapid Evolution of Scholarly Communication." *Learned Publishing* 15, no.1 (2002): 7–19. Also to appear in *Bits and Bucks: Economics and Usage of Digital Collections,* ed. W. Lougee and J. MacKie-Mason. Cambridge, Mass.: MIT Press, 2002. Available online at www.dtc.umn.edu/~odlyzko/doc/rapid.evolution.pdf.

WILL E-PUBLISHING
SAVE ACADEMIC RESEARCH?

Originally published October 1999

Questions like the one above should be discouraged. They mask complexity and promote monothetic thinking, where messiness and emergence are the order of the day. As my colleagues Rob Kling and Geoff McKim (1999) observed, much of the extensive literature on e-publishing "homogenizes the character of publishing." So, let's begin with a quick deconstruction of e-publishing. Different disciplinary communities have different understandings of what it means to publish and be published. That has long been the case. The social and material practices that constitute e-publishing in high-energy physics, molecular biology, cultural studies, and law are quite distinct. Interestingly, cross-field variations are largely independent of the highly visible tools and technologies associated with electronic publishing. Common platforms don't breed common approaches. Rather, publishing practices and expectations within a given research community are shaped by prevailing norms and conventions. Nothing new in that. Traditionally, a refereed conference paper has counted for something in computer science, but is likely to be given short shrift by a promotion and tenure committee in a business school. A monograph (preferably one published by a reputable university press) will be expected of a junior scholar in English, but not of an aspiring mathematician. This being so, our pronouncements about publishing really should be grounded in the multiple realities of tribal life in academe.

The success of Paul Ginsparg's (xxx.lanl.gov:80/Welcome.html) innovative physics electronic preprint archive (and its replication in a number of other fields) doesn't mean that this model should, or will, become standard. What works for high energy physics and some other domains may not work for researchers in cultural anthropology or medieval history. Disciplines differ significantly in terms of their sociocognitive structures, degrees of paradigmatic consensus, funding mechanisms, collaborative intensity, and institutionalized quality assurance mechanisms. It would be naïve to expect uniform adoption profiles. For instance, the policies of professional associations, such as the ACM (Association for Computing Machinery), ACS (American Chemical Society), APA (American Psychological Association), differ with regard to electronic posting and publishing. In many fields, long-established (and medium-independent) modes of peer review will continue to be of pivotal importance. Looking ahead, various strains of "peer review lite" may prove acceptable for certain purposes and constituencies, with inclusion in the journal (or e-archive) of record still requiring full-blown peer review. In any event, there is no logical reason, as Stevan Harnad (www.princeton.edu/~harnad/intpub.html) and others (*Policy Perspectives*) have argued, why peer review can't be decoupled entirely from the business of journal publishing. Trust (between publishing scholars), trustworthiness (of institutional arrangements, such as the peer review process), and credibility (a journal's pedigree and reputation) are the essential glues that hold the primary communication system in place. These will persist. None of the quiddities and practices sketched above, however, should deter us from making a few more or less plausible claims about e-publishing and its likely impact on academic research.

First, e-publishing increases the velocity of communication, such that the time-to-market for new ideas and research results is shortened appreciably. That is good news all around. Funding agencies see the fruits of their investment earlier, and authors get into print more quickly. As a result, the printed journal is no longer a current awareness, but an archival medium, at best. Second, consortial licensing agreements in networked environments have opened up vast e-journal collections to a wider audience than would otherwise have been the case (the OhioLINK/Academic Press and Cal State/EBSCO package deals are illustrative of the trend). Again, a positive sum outcome: publishers, librarians, scholars, and students are better off than before, though there remains the sensitive issue of sustainable (transgenerational) access to publishers' digital archives. Third, the economics of scholarly publishing are set to change (though exactly how, when, and to what extent remain hotly contested issues). This is presumably good news for institutional purchasers (a.k.a. librarians) who are angered by excessive journal price hikes, but not such good news for profiteering publishers. The relative rising cost of ST&M (scientific, technological, and medical) journals compared with the CPI (consumer price index) is a cause of much lamentation, though not everyone takes the ARL's (Association of Research Libraries) data at face value. Andrew Odlyzko notes (www.research.att.com/~amo/doc/competition.cooperation.txt) with impish seriousness that some research libraries spend just over a third of their operating budgets on library materials; commercial publishers know full well that there is still some fat on the institutional bone! E-publishing should also be good news for humanities scholars covetous of tenure who fear the demise of the university press and with it the seemingly last opportunity to publish high-quality, limited appeal monographs. Even better news is the willingness of some university presses, such as Columbia (Wittenberg 1998), to explore new ways of presenting scholarship and stimulating on-line debate.

Fourth, e-publishing makes vertical integration a real possibility for would-be scholars/publishers (and their parent institutions). If SPARC (Scholarly Publishing & Academic Resources Coalition) grows significantly, invites imitators, or spawns variations on the initial theme, some commercial publishers will be less than thrilled. E-publishing has also triggered a wave of experimentation and collaboration (JSTOR, HighWire, BioOne, Project Muse, and the NIH's [National Institutes of Health] proposed PubMed Central are early examples), which is good news for the scholarly community, learned societies, and their individual members but, ultimately, not such good news for some commercial publishers. From these protobusiness models, new forms of customized and cost-competitive service provision will surely evolve. Fifth, e-publishing has engendered new modes of digital communication and discourse. Scholarly skywriting, to use Harnad's cute coinage, is an appropriately postmodern construct. Version follows version; commentaries pile on top of commentaries. The age of promiscuous publishing and the electronic palimpsest ("stretch text") has dawned. Proponents of open peer review take pride in counterpointing the limitations of the classic peer review process (embarrassingly weak levels of inter-referee agreement for starters) with the transparency and robustness of digital debate. It's Gresham's Law in reverse. Sixth, e-publishing is credited with democratizing a process that, heretofore, has been controlled by elites; producer-led innovation has been a striking feature of first generation Web-based publishing. Consequently, mavericks, marginals, and the historically disenfranchised (many Third World researchers, for example) now have their voice, though, of course, there's no guarantee that the elites are listening.

Developments in e-publishing are convulsing the scholarly communication ecosystem. New players, new relationships, new products, new distribution channels, new pricing mechanisms, new rules. Things ain't what they used to be. And it's certainly not clear what lies ahead. Forecasting is fun, but futile. Suffice it to say that innovation and experimentation will continue apace, and that the balance of power between authors, publishers, and consumers has altered irrevocably. New models will emerge, mutate, and fade way, only to be replaced rapidly by others. Given the diversity of stakeholders and heterogeneity of culturally validated practices, it would be foolish to imagine that a monolithic e-publishing model or system could emerge. Pluralism, plasticity, and adaptivity will be hallmarks of the new world order. Despite all the uncertainties, I, for one, am sanguine about the future of academic research, given the enormous flexibility and efficiencies afforded by e-publishing.

REFERENCES

Kling, R., and G. McKim. "Scholarly Communication and the Continuum of Electronic Publishing." *Journal of the American Society for Information Science* 50, no. 10 (1999): 890–906.

"To Publish and Perish." *Policy Perspectives* 7, no. 4 (1999): 1–11.

Wittenberg, K. "Cutting-Edge Scholarship and Electronic Publishing." *The Chronicle of Higher Education* (June 19, 1998): B6.

Acknowledged but Ignored: Credit Where Credit's Due

Originally published February 1992

Even bodybuilders fret less about their vital statistics than we academics do. We are forever sizing one another up; evaluating resumes, reviewing dossiers, ranking productivity, rating scholarship. Vita building has become the academic equivalent of the workout. We measure what we can (publications, citations, teaching scores, grant awards, honors, fellowships, invited presentations, etc.). Take citation counting.

The pros and cons of the approach have been aired exhaustively and don't need to be rolled out again; suffice to say that all citations—substantive, perfunctory, negative or whatever—are treated as equal, though some are clearly more equal than others. The citing of one author by another is treated as a significant event in communication terms, and the more significant events recorded in favor of a particular author, the greater that author's presumed influence or prestige. As a consequence, citations have acquired convertible currency status in the evaluation process; to be highly cited is to become hot property.

So far so good. But citation counts are an incomplete register of influence. There are other significant "events" that warrant attention. Like acknowledgment. How often do we read at the end of a journal article something like the following: "I am indebted to my colleagues X and Y who read early drafts of this paper and made many valuable comments and suggestions"? What are we to make of such acknowledgments to the contributions of a trusted assessor, mentor, or advisor? As things stand, being mentioned in the acknowledgments coda to a scholarly article (or doctoral dissertation or monograph, for that matter) is to be consigned to limbo. In the prevailing reward system of science, the acknowledgment has no status, no cash-in value. And here's the rub: while a glowing acknowledgment counts for naught, a negative citation still sets the register ringing. Such a position is logically inconsistent.

It's time to take acknowledgments seriously and consider how citations and acknowledgments could be used conjointly in the assessment of both individual and institutional research performance. Many articles carry acknowledgments. These can range from a one-line expression of gratitude to a graduate assistant to a paragraph-length statement acknowledging a multiplicity of influences. Many articles carry compound acknowledgments, reflecting a mix of personal, moral, financial, technical, and conceptual support from institutions, agencies, coworkers, and peers.

To get a feel for the practice, I recently analyzed all acknowledgment statements attached to research articles appearing in the *Journal of the American Society for Information Science* over a twenty-year period. Almost half (444 articles) carried an acknowledgment of some kind; almost a quarter (244) made explicit reference to intellectual input (inspiration, guidance, critical comment, feedback, etc.) received from peers, mentors, or coworkers (420 names in all). Most of these individuals (85 percent) were mentioned once; only twenty-five received three or more mentions. This, of course, is just the kind of concentration we have come to expect in analyzing the distribution of citations; citation and acknowledgment stars are equally thin on the ground.

If the results of this exploratory survey are anything to go by, many researchers take seriously the task of discharging their intellectual debts via acknowledgments—just as seriously as citing the appropriate works in the reference lists and bibliographies that accompany their publications. This raises a number of interesting issues and questions: (a) what is the degree of correlation between cited and acknowledged authors; are we dealing with identical, overlapping, or discrete populations? (b) is there a hidden population of influencers whose contributions as nurturers, stimulators, and mentors does not show up on publication and citation counts? (c) why are these explicit expressions of intellectual debt not treated and processed like citations? (d) why does the humble acknowledgment not feature in the academic auditor's armamentarium; why does it not play a part in the tenure review process? (e) what are the norms of acknowledgment? (f) could the protocols and practice of acknowledgment be standardized (the equivalent of a referencing house style) so that acknowledgment counting, like citation counting, would be amenable to automation? (g) what are the financial and practical constraints to producing, say, an acknowledgment index, comparable with, and complementary to, the Institute for Information Science (ISI) *Science Citation Index*?

In many cases, the acknowledgment functions as a kind of closet citation. It almost begs to be taken out, dusted down, and put to good use. Those who are concerned about equity in the context of the promotion and tenure process would do well to consider how existing indicators might be bolstered by the introduction of data on acknowledgment frequency. On the surface, there is a compelling case for taking a fresh look at the social and cognitive significance of acknowledgments in the primary communication process. (For a comprehensive treatment of this topic, see Blaise Cronin, *The Scholar's Courtesy: The Role of Acknowledgement in the Primary Communication Process* [London: Taylor Graham, 1995]).

New Age Numerology: A Gloss on Apostol

Originally published June 1998

A little context is required here. I was asked by the editors of Science Tribune, *a French electronic journal, if I would respond to an article by Marian Apostol, a Romanian theoretical physicist, on the current obsession for auditing and measuring scientific activity and output (www.tribunes.com /tribune/art98/apo2.htm). Apostol's lively polemic tilts at "nonsensical, money-oriented neurasthenic science" and takes a swipe or two at bibliometricians, who, in his view, "are not interested in what is written in a paper because they have no means of counting the worth of an article." Below is my brief riposte.*

Make no mistake about it, bibliometricians invite lampoonery. Their parasitic craft is emblematic of all that is awry in our postmodern world, with its Alice in Wonderland sense of logic and fetishistic attachment to accountability. We reward these wannabe metascientists, these counters of glass beads, while punishing real scientists for not being widely enough published or cited. The tail is now wagging the scientific dog. In recent years, the science policy community has constructed a virtual panopticon policed by thuggish bibliometricians and sundry others to monitor the performance of career scientists. It's all such a very long way from the halcyon days of the seventeenth century, where gentlemen scientists and civil processes of authentication were the order of the day (Shapin 1994), and where the notion of science for science's sake (*l'art pour l'art*) was uncontested. How Boyle and Cavendish must be turning in their graves, and Foucault smiling. For Apostol, this metric madness calls to mind the medieval schoolmen's tortuous wrangling about the number of angels on a pinhead. Now the pinheads, so to speak, are responsible for evaluating men of science. The obscenity of this inversion is too much for Apostol, and he slips from lampoonery into unsavory caricature of all things bibliometric.

But science is not a world apart. In so many walks of late twentieth-century life, be it medicine, financial services, or government, the demand for accountability from taxpayers and their elected representatives has become institutionalized. Scientists are only one of several elite professional groups who recently have found themselves under the microscope and seen their autonomy eroded. Why shouldn't federal agencies, research councils, national academies of science, and similar organizations take reasonable steps to ensure that their funds are efficiently and effectively disbursed? The case for the systematic gathering of data on researchers' performance and productivity to ensure that society derives maximal benefit from the national science budget is a "no brainer," as Americans would say, though not, apparently, for Apostol, who believes that intrinsic value and individual creativity should drive scientific inquiry. It's not for him, the customer-contractor model for commissioning applied science, which became so popular in the early 1970s (Kogan and Henkel 1983). But the reality is, there are no more free lunches. Instead, lunch tokens are required—in the shape of results, outcomes, and impacts and, of course, the associated array of bibliometric (and other) indicators by which these effects can be quantified. For good or ill, the discourse of science policy mirrors that of management and market research. Talk of "picking winners" is near and dear to ministerial hearts. We now speak of France's market share of the world's high energy physics research, as reflected in publications and citations (Irvine and Martin 1984), just as we would of its share of the fine wine market. *Autres temps, autres moeurs.*

Of course, there is the not-so-trivial problem of fraud in science (Altman 1997). Can the growing reports of scientific misconduct (fabrication, falsification, plagiarism) continue to be swept under the carpet, or is it time to expose and document the scale of the phenomenon? As Ben-Yehuda (1986, 17) noted more than a decade ago, "There exists a bitter argument whether deviance in science is better represented by the 'iceberg theory' or by 'the bad apples' theory." Apostol goes for the few bad apples theory, but I remember the *Titanic*. And that makes me much less cavalier than he when it comes to peer review, flawed though the system undeniably is (Chubin and Hackett 1990). Peer review, to paraphrase Winston Churchill on democracy, is the least worst of the options available. But it also works remarkably well in some contexts. Think of high energy physics, where the internal peer review conducted by members of the different collaborations (e.g., CLAS, PHOBOS) and institutions (e.g., CERN, FERMILAB) is so intense and carefully choreographed (see www.physics.odu.edu/~dodge/charter_jan98.txt) that preprints have acquired the assured authority of articles in the traditional printed journal of record—as Ginsparg and colleagues at Los Alamos have demonstrated with their e-print exchange. Moreover, without peer review, Fleischmann and Pons might still be peddling the idea of cold fusion to the state of Utah and other equally gullible would-be backers (Close 1990). Here was a relatively rare occasion when the global scientific community needed no persuading to replicate an experiment.

And herein lies the pivotal issue. The stakes involved in Big Science are enormous. Dollars and reputations are on the line; the winner takes all. Given the intensity of the race for scientific breakthroughs, there is little incentive for career scientists to undertake replication studies. The reward system favors novelty and, consequently, the market for reproducible results is almost nonexistent (Feigenbaum and Levy 1993). However, incentives for replication would reduce spurious knowledge claims and deter malfeasance. As things stand, the scientific reward system is massively skewed in favor of originality, not rigor. This is where change ought to be effected. In choosing soft targets, such as evaluative bibliometrics and peer review, Apostol has foregone an opportunity to stimulate meaningful discussion.

REFERENCES

Altman, E. "Scientific Research Misconduct." In *Research Misconduct: Issues, Implications and Strategies*, ed. E. Altman and P. Hernon, 1–31. Greenwich, Conn.: Ablex, 1997.

Ben-Yehuda, N. "Deviance in Science." *British Journal of Criminology* 26 (January 1986): 1–27.

Chubin, D. E., and E. J. Hackett. *Peerless Science: Peer Review and U.S. Science Policy*. Albany: SUNY Press, 1990.

Close, F. *Too Hot to Handle: The Race for Cold Fusion*. London: Allen, 1990.

Feigenbaum, S., and D. M. Levy. "The Market for (Ir)Reproducible Econometrics." *Social Epistemology* 7, no. 3 (1993): 215–32.

Irvine, J., and B. R. Martin. *Foresight in Science: Picking the Winners*. London: Pinter, 1984.

Kogan, M., and M. Henkel. *Government and Research: The Rothschild Experiment in a Government Department*. London: Heinemann, 1983.

Shapin, S. *A Social History of Truth*. Chicago, Ill.: University of Chicago Press, 1994.

THE WARHOLIAN MOMENT
AND OTHER PROTO-INDICATORS
OF SCHOLARLY SALIENCE

Originally published 1999

NEW MEDIA

The acceptability of electronic publications for academic promotion and tenure (P&T) purposes has been a subject of lively discussion in recent years (Cronin and Overfelt 1995). Tenure-seeking scholars have repeatedly expressed concerns that publishing in non-traditional outlets or media could be detrimental to their career development, as e-journals and other electronic fora may lack pedigree and legitimacy in the eyes of P&T review panel members. Some of these concerns may be real, some imagined. However, with the inexorable rise of electronic publishing, and evolving forms of online peer review, it seems inevitable that tolerance of digital media will become the norm and that these fears will fade.

NEW MORES

This leads on to a related issue. If, in fact, alternative publishing practices and media are admissible for P&T purposes, might we expect to see a concomitant broadening of the criteria used to assess the many ways in which academic influence is exercised and subsequently acknowledged? Might novel indicators of scholarly salience and impact be factored into established evaluation processes to take account of shifting social practices and values? This question was raised recently by Brown-Sayed (1999): "Are people counting hits on their web sites and their articles in ejournals for P&T purposes? If so, do they 'count'?"

This same issue was addressed tangentially by Cronin et al. (1998) in an early study of invocation on the World Wide Web. They identified a wide variety of ways and contexts in which scholars and their work were mentioned on the Web. They also correlated frequency of mention with citation counts to see whether highly cited scholars also had high Web visibility. However, they cautioned against using an individual's "presence density" on the Web as a partial proxy for scholarly impact or esteem, given serious concerns about the reliability of the data produced by commercial search engines (Snyder and Rosenbaum 1999).

NEW MEASURES

The questions, nonetheless, are worth keeping on the table. Suppose search engine reliability were not an issue, what kinds of complementary measures could be harvested on the Web that might usefully inform the P&T process? Some more or less plausible candidates come quickly to mind—citations on another researcher's Web page, for example, or having one's publications listed in a professor's online syllabus. The first of these is a classic measure and all that's different is the fact that the citation in this instance is to be found on an individual's Web page and not in the pages of a traditional, peer-reviewed publication, be it printed or electronic. These stepchild citations could be introduced into the P&T process as supplementary evidence of a scholar's impact on the wider professional community, though, perhaps, given less weight. The second category of invocation is a potentially useful indicator of how an individual's research and thinking have percolated into the classroom, a perfectly legitimate extension of the evaluative frame, since teaching quality is (in theory, if not always in practice) a central aspect in determining promotability and tenurability.

Other measures are less conventional, but certainly deserving of consideration. Think of an individual whose ideas or theories are the cynosure of an extended listserv discussion within his or her peer community. Arguably, that in itself is an expression of perceived, if transient, utility or merit—whether the ideas are being lauded or rebutted. At present, there is no convenient or credible way of logging or accommodating this kind of "scholarly skywriting" (Harnad 1990) in traditional faculty evaluations. It could be argued that the P&T process is already prolix and burdensome enough without adding yet more (and untried) variables to the evaluative mix, but that would be myopic. The Web is a fertile domain for scholarly expression and communication (Cronin and McKim 1996) and emergent forms of recognition, acknowledgment, and approbation at least deserve to be documented and their social significance analyzed before being dismissed as invalid or supernumerary.

MAKING A SPLASH

Then there are putative indicators that might just be expected to raise a scholarly eyebrow or two—raw counts of hits to a researcher's Web page. Here, a little caution is warranted. Convenient and appealing though such "splash factors" (Brown-Sayed 1999) might be, they would likely be of limited value. As the commercial market research community is only too well aware, there is a big difference between a consumer eyeballing a company's Web-based advertising on a portal site and hyperlinking to that company's Web page. Crude hits are much less useful measures than click-through rates in terms of assessing an advertisement's effectiveness—hence the growing interest in performance-based advertising (Gurley 1998). Analogously, hit rates to a scholar's home page should not be construed uncritically as surrogates of impact or quality, but as, at most, preliminary indicators of possible impact.

Adler (1999) has quantified what he calls the "slashdot effect," the seemingly spontaneous hit rate logged by a server following an announcement or posting of a story on a high-volume news website. He plotted the hit rate per minute for three stories published on *Slashdot*, *Linux Today*, and *Freshmeat* and found dramatic surge effects in each case. As in academe, so in the marketplace. Something comparable seems to have happened following Victoria's Secret's advertising during the 1999 Superbowl: hits to its website surged such that access degraded dramatically, a problem experienced, too, by Hotjobs.com, another first-time Superbowl advertiser. Whether, and to what extent, these companies' profitability has been boosted by their TV advertising (and the associated Web spill-over) remains to be seen. From an academic perspective, the question is whether the slashdot effect signifies a flash in the critical pan, or constitutes a leading indicator of scholarly impact.

SURGE SIGNIFICANCE

Wisely, Adler drew no inference about readership levels (let alone impact or quality) from the data in his study. It would, however, be intriguing to know whether the short-lived surge in hits to the three stories he tracked translated over time into follow-up actions, such as downloading of files or, ultimately, reading and citing the works in question. In other words, are we looking at essentially superficial and herdlike behaviors which testify little, if at all, to cognitive enrichment, or should we assume that surging leads to greater likelihood of a scholar's ideas being digested and incorporated into the mainstream literature?

If anything, this kind of swarming behavior seems likely to intensify as recommender systems proliferate, and the numbers of pointers and links in circulation at any given moment grows. But readers' time and attention are limited; the indiscriminate follower of others' recommendations may end up skimming and grazing in such a way that texts are rarely engaged with in meaningful fashion. In most cases, surge-activating papers will presumably exhibit very short and near-perpendicular life-cycle curves (so different from the typical life-cycle curve associated with a journal article's citation profile), as transient group interest races to the next hot item, creating a digital age equivalent of Andy Warhol's fifteen minutes of fame for Web-present authors.

CONCLUSION

If some of the approaches above are to be considered as supplementary sources of data for P&T committees and academic evaluators in general, then it is important that the preferred measures can demonstrate requisite validity and reliability, not to mention some degree of utility. While a high hit rate may briefly create a feel-good effect for the author, there is no guarantee that the work in question will prove to have staying power. A Web-accessible article that generates a high splash factor may, of course, turn out to be a highly influential paper, but there is no necessary reason to assume such. Much remains unclear about the kinds of emergent practices and proto-indicators sketched in this note and their longer-term import within the academic evaluation context, but, here, surely is an issue ripe for systematic scrutiny.

REFERENCES

Adler, S. "The Slashdot Effect: An Analysis of Three Internet Publications," 1999. Available at: http://ssadler.phy.bnl.gov/adler/SDE/SlashDotEffect .html (accessed August 15, 2002).

Brown-Sayed, C. "E-hits and Tenure?" Open Lib/Info Sci Education Forum, 1999. JESSE@UTKVM1.UTK.EDU, 5 February.

Cronin, B., and K. Overfelt. "E-journals and Tenure." *Journal of the American Society for Information Science* 46, no. 9 (1995): 700–703.

Cronin, B., and G. McKim. "Science and Scholarship on the World Wide Web: A North American Perspective." *Journal of Documentation* 52, no. 2 (1996): 163–71.

Cronin, B., H. W. Snyder, H. Rosenbaum, A. Martinson, and E. Callahan. "Invoked on the Web." *Journal of the American Society for Information Science* 49, no. 14 (1998): 1319–28.

Gurley, W. "How the Web Will Warp Advertising." *Fortune* (November 9, 1998): 119–20.

Harnad, S. "Scholarly Skywriting and the Prepublication Continuum of Scientific Inquiry." *Psychological Science* 1 (1990): 342–43.

Snyder, H., and H. Rosenbaum. "Can Search Engines Be Used as Tools for Web-link Analysis? A Critical View." *Journal of Documentation* 55, no.4 (1999): 185–89.

ABOUT THE AUTHOR

Blaise Cronin is the Rudy Professor of Information Science at Indiana University, Bloomington, where he has been dean of the School of Library and Information Science since 1991. He is concurrently a Visiting Professor in the School of Computing at Napier University, Edinburgh, and Visiting Professor of Information Science at Manchester Metropolitan University. From 1985 to 1991, he was Professor of Information Science and head of the Department of Information Science at the Strathclyde University Business School in Glasgow.

Professor Cronin is the author/editor of some 300 research articles, monographs, technical reports, conference papers, and other publications. In addition, he has published numerous book reviews. Much of his research focuses on scholarly communication, citation analysis, scientometrics, and cybermetrics—the intersection of information science and social studies of science. He has also published extensively on topics such as information warfare, strategic intelligence, knowledge management, information marketing, distributed education, and the social dimensions of digitization. Professor Cronin is editor of the *Annual Review of Information Science and Technology* (ARIST), which is published by the American Society for Information Science and Technology. He was founding editor of the *Journal of Economic & Social Intelligence* and sits on many editorial boards, including *Cybermetrics*, *Journal of the American Society for Information Science & Technology*, *International Journal of Information Management*, *Information Research*, *Library Quarterly*, and *Scientometrics*.

Professor Cronin has extensive international experience, having taught, conducted research, or consulted in more than thirty countries; clients have included the World Bank, Asian Development Bank, UNESCO, Brazilian Ministry of Science & Technology, European

Commission, U.S. Department of Justice, British Council, Her Majesty's Treasury, Hewlett-Packard, British Library, Commonwealth Agricultural Bureau, and Association for Information Management. He has been a keynote or invited speaker at scores of conferences, nationally and internationally. Professor Cronin was a founding director of Crossaig, an electronic publishing start-up in Scotland, which was acquired in 1992 by ISI (Institute for Scientific Information) in Philadelphia. For six years, he was a member of ISI's strategic advisory board.

Professor Cronin was educated at Trinity College Dublin (M.A.) and the Queen's University of Belfast (M.L.S., Ph.D., D.S.Sc.). In 1997, he was awarded the degree Doctor of Letters (D.Litt., *honoris causa*) by Queen Margaret University College, Edinburgh, for his scholarly contributions to information science. Professor Cronin is a Fellow of the Institute of Information Scientists, Royal Society of Arts, Institute of Management, and the Library Association.